Back to the future

PHILIP COOKE

University of Wales
College of Cardiff

London
UNWIN HYMAN
Boston Sydney Wellington

Published by the Academic Division of
Unwin Hyman Ltd
15/17 Broadwick Street, London W1V 1FP, UK

Unwin Hyman Inc.,
8 Winchester Place, Winchester, Mass. 01890, USA

Allen & Unwin (Australia) Ltd,
8 Napier Street, North Sydney, NSW 2060, Australia

Allen & Unwin (New Zealand) Ltd in association with the
Port Nicholson Press Ltd,
Compusales Building, 75 Ghuznee Street, Wellington 1, New Zealand

First published in 1990

British Library Cataloguing in Publication Data

Cooke, P. N. (Philip Nicholas), *1946–*
Back to the future: Modernity, postmodernity and locality.
1. Western culture. Modernism & postmodernism
I. Title
306
ISBN 0–04–445586–0

Library of Congress Cataloging in Publication Data

Data applied for

Data converted to 10/13 Palatino by Columns of Reading
and printed in Great Britain
by Billing & Son Ltd, London & Worcester

Contents

Contents

Acknowledgements

This book arose from the Economic and Social Research Council's Research Programme into 'The Changing Urban and Regional System in the United Kingdom'. This was a study carried out from 1984 to 1987 of the ways in which economic restructuring had impacted upon localities in the UK and how those localities had responded to or anticipated such change, to their advantage or disadvantage. The question of local initiative and innovation was uppermost in the minds of those researchers taking part in the study. In writing this book I am grateful for the remarkable contribution made by the seven study teams whom I co-ordinated. They were based in the Gloucester College of Advanced Technology, the Centre of Environmental Studies, London, the University of Kent at Canterbury, the University of Bristol, the University of Aston in Birmingham, the University of Lancaster, and the University of Durham.

For helping me formulate the ideas which have informed this book I am particularly grateful to the Academic Board of the University of Utrecht who, by inviting me to take the Belle van Zuyl chair in Geography as a Visiting Professor, enabled me to find the time to write the book. Frans Dieleman and Jan van Weesep deserve special thanks. For discussing questions of modernity and locality with me, I would like to thank John Urry, Derek Gregory, Susan

Acknowledgements

Christopherson, Ed Soja, Michael Storper, Mike Featherstone, Niels Albertsen, Scott Lash, Giaocchino Garofoli, George Marcus, Allen Scott, Nigel Thrift, Alain Lipietz, Rob Shields, Erik Swyngedouw, Anne Knudsen, Irena Onufrijchuk, Peter Dickens, Ben Janssen and Vincente Granados. For the pleasure of their company while writing this book, I would like to thank Peter Hooimeyer and Ton van Rietbergen.

PHILIP COOKE

Utrecht

December 1988

*for Nia, Lowri, Lleucu
and Catrin*

Introduction

'Postmodernist' is the name that has come to be applied to those who challenge the intellectual and aesthetic inheritance of modernity. The label is surrounded by controversy. Those who accept it can appear subversive, hedonistic and playful. Critics see postmodernists as superficial, populist and enslaved by mass-media imagery. They accuse them of being neoconservative in culture and politics. They say they are not serious about any moral basis to what they seek to express. The question of whether modernity is being replaced by an opposite culture of postmodernity is the subject of this book.

Living in interesting times can be exhilarating but also disconcerting. As the twentieth-century *fin de siècle* approaches we seem to be confronted by change wherever we look. Debates about future directions have been raging throughout the 1980s. Some of these debates have filled the columns of the press and the air time of radio and television on an almost daily basis. Is the market the best mechanism for determining the allocation of all goods and services? Should the welfare state be dismantled? Are rising crime figures the result of unemployment, the breakdown of the family, or the inadequacy of the courts, the police, the prisons, society itself? Is there such a thing as society, or are there just families and individuals? If individuals are free to choose and benefit from the products and services of the market, do they also have responsibilities towards other individuals less able to choose? Does private affluence necessarily mean public squalor? What is to be done about the condition of our cities, roads, railways? Why did we build high-rise flats? Was modern architecture a mistake?

These debates have often engaged surprising protagonists. In Britain members of the government have found themselves locked in controversy with leading members of the church, the monarchy and the media. A report produced by the Archbishop of Canterbury's special commission on the plight of cities was dismissed by a government minister as Marxist propaganda. A member of the royal family was attacked by another minister for not having a proper job. The same member of the monarchy has launched a campaign against modern architecture. Other members of the royal family are known to be critical of government policies towards the unemployed.

This book attempts to explain the problems that underlie such debates. It argues that modernity itself is in some ways a cause of the contradictions that plague it. A key contradiction is between the new value of individualism and those older values that bonded people in communities. For the past 150 years the tension between these values was successfully held in check. Developments within the modern nation-state allowed free reign to the individual while protecting from exploitation those lacking in money, schooling and expertise. In the 1980s the contradictions have become overwhelming. The hawsers that once held the two positions together have snapped.

Such tensions have not been released in political and social affairs alone. We live in an era when the methods of scientific and technological progress have come under fire, not only for their apparent indifference to social improvement and environmental degradation, but also for their apparent uninterest in ethical questions posed by their discoveries. In the aesthetic sphere there has been a major

Figure 1 Unlikely combatants in the battle of modern values.

questioning of the principles and ideals which underpinned modernism in literature, music, painting and, above all, architecture. Some have argued that modernism is exhausted, others that the Enlightenment, which led to the emancipation of thought from the clutches of religious dogma, is itself exhausted and that modernity, defined as a commitment to live by the rules of reason rather than of superstition, has come to an end. Others, who fear that such a claim heralds a dark age of barbarism, predict a war of all against all with victory going to the loudest shouter, and struggle to retain a hold on the progressive ideals of modernity. Still others seem to want to wish away the history of the twentieth century and return to a revived classical era of aesthetic conservatism and philosophical certainty.

In this book it is argued that postmodernism in its many guises is more of an internal critique of modernism, and the interpretation of reason embodied in modernity, than an attempt totally to subvert it. If postmodernism has an objective, which some have doubted, it is to criticize the advocates of modernity for what they leave out and what they stress. In other words, postmodernism is the continuation of modernism by other means.

Postmodernists argue that modern perspectives undervalue, amongst other things, the concerns of minorities, local identities, non-western thinking, a capacity to deal with difference, the pluralist culture and the cosmopolitanism of modern life. Much attention is paid to the implications of this critique in this book. Substantial parts of it are devoted to the contradictions between centralized power in government, the economy and culture, and the local settings in which, for the most part, everyday life is carried out. Special emphasis is placed upon the ways in which local perspectives are making themselves felt against the constraints of centralized power as it operates in the regions and cities of contemporary society. In particular urban society in Britain is explored by examining the global as well as the national forces responsible for the growing divisions between the depressed north and the booming south, the deprived inner cities and the affluent suburbs, the struggling, deindustrialized localities and the successful, not to say complacent, localities of the contemporary period.

Sustaining this investigation is an account of highly significant changes underway in the practices of business, large and small, and the impacts these changes are having upon towns and cities. In the discussion recourse is made to a helpful way of thinking about business organization which emphasizes the method of mass-production pioneered by the Ford Motor Corporation. It is shown that the innovations made in Detroit in the early years of the twentieth century had far-reaching implications for business organization throughout the world. But, more importantly, 'Fordism' – to use the shorthand – had major implications for the economic management systems installed in the modern western economies in which Keynesian policy instruments became a major factor in trying to maintain a balance between mass production and mass consumption. It is the breakdown of Fordism, in association with the rejection in many advanced countries of Keynesianism, that has helped create the crisis to which neoconservative politics has been one response. I argue that from the business point of view we have entered a post-Fordist period in which, intriguingly, there is a new emphasis upon co-operation (though that does not by any means imply the demise of competition), a revaluation of local discourses and, indeed, localities as key building blocks of the newer forms of economic organization.

The book is divided into two parts. The first half explores the nature of modernity and the ways in which its characteristic modes of thinking, discourse and practice coalesced with but also replaced those that preceded it. The second half examines the various social, cultural, political and economic forces that have been ranged, some would say, *against* the project of modernity, though my argument is that they have the effect of renewing it. The first chapter of the book examines the psychology of the modern experience as older, rural lifestyles gave way to the more fleeting and fragmentary experiences of modern urban life in the great industrial cities that were modernity's first and lasting symbolic contribution to history. The discussion then turns to the emergence of the aesthetic norms and cultural standards of modernism and its changing, even contradictory relationships with classicism, romanticism and realism. This is followed by an account of the formation of the modern state, particularly the making of national identities, and the Janus-faced character of the process, keeping one foot securely in the past while placing the other in the uncertainties of a future that was being actively produced. Here some comparisons are also drawn with the experience of aesthetic modernism.

The second chapter explores the fate of community as both a concept and a reality of the era of modernity. The argument is developed that community in the sense of a co-operative, kin and family-based authority system was always on the defensive in the face of modern individualism and the concept of the sovereign modern state. The idea of community is shown to have informed a great deal of intellectual activity as thinkers who sought to explain both change and stability in the social and legal order struggled to unite the incompatible. It is proposed that community now largely persists as a symbolic or mythical element of contemporary culture, signified most poignantly in the widespread attempt to re-appropriate popular, communal experiences in the form of the modern museum exhibit and even the modern theme park.

Chapter 3 examines the ways in which modern factory production, based on the highly differentiated division of labour and the separation of conception from execution of the work task enabled modern capitalism to expand enormously into a system capable of serving mass markets rather than simply local or regional ones. The principles of the modern factory system are outlined and the interaction between mass production and mass consumption is interpreted through the forms it took in the development of the modern system of cities and regions. The chapter ends with an analysis of the internal contradictions of Fordism and an explanation of its demise as a major business 'discourse' or set of assumptions about the optimum way in which to organize production.

Chapter 4 broaches the question of postmodernity. It consists of an account of the manner in which aesthetic modernism has come under attack from diverse angles. This then leads into a consideration of important disagreements about the crisis of philosophy, the nature of knowledge, and the methods appropriate to generating it. The chapter then moves back into the cultural sphere with an examination of the postmodern critique and its alternative perspectives in the spheres of contemporary fiction-writing and 'postmodern' architecture. An assessment is then presented of criticisms that have been advanced against postmodernism itself.

One of the important proposals of postmodern thought is that local knowledge, identity and activity have been under-theorised in modern discourse. Chapter 5 explores the spatial or geographical dimension of this question by focusing on a detailed study of changes under way in the British urban and regional system. It is argued that local differences are expanding and that local consciousness and social innovation centred upon a renewed idea of citizenship are pressing hard against modern forms of centralist political control. A rejuvenated concept of 'locality', echoing a reassertion of spatial issues in social science, is key to this development.

The sixth chapter focuses back on economic affairs, paying special attention to the somewhat surprising outbreak of co-operation, incorporation and reinterpretation of the local specificities of workforces and business linkages that are observable as companies seek to survive in an ever harsher competitive environment. The post-Fordist era signifies a recognition of the growing importance of local–global economic relations as some of the traditional powers of the modern nation state weaken somewhat. Then, in a concluding chapter, the implications of these changes for new kinds of local cultural, political and social welfare activities are traced.

CHAPTER ONE

The question of modernity

Modern life

We all think we know what it is to be modern. To have a modern kitchen means to have a number of machines and gadgets to do what our parents or grandparents used to do by hand. A washing machine is the perfect emblem of modernity. Previously clothes had to be collected, water had to be boiled, stains had to be rubbed out energetically with a bar of soap on a washing board, semi-washed clothes had to be put in the boiler, clean clothes had to be put through the mangle, then the whole lot had to be pegged out on a line or spread over hedges to dry. Now the machine can do everything except peg the clothes out, and if it has an in-built tumble dryer even the pegging out is unnecessary.

A modern car is probably one that has a smooth, aerodynamic profile, adjustable seats and steering wheel, a centrally-controlled, anti-theft locking system, electronically-controlled side windows, demisting devices, a heater, air conditioning, anti-lock braking, an automatic gearbox, digital speedometer and other information systems, an electronic, stereo radio and tape deck, perhaps an on-board computer which monitors engine performance and a virtually unerodable body finish. This is not only different in terms of safety and comfort from the Model T Ford, once considered the acme of modernity, but different from the Vauxhall Victor of the 1960s. In some ways there were more similarities

1

between those two models than between the Victor and today's Cavalier. Heaters, radios, safety belts, some of the dials were optional extras on most of the cars of the 60s. Their bodywork eroded in record time, their suspension was spongy, their engines under-powered and dramatically thirsty, they were spine-bendingly uncomfortable in many cases, and available only in a limited range of styles.

What today, is a modern lifestyle? Depending upon age and marital status, it will contain the expectation of reasonable income, if not some wealth – particularly in the bricks and mortar of the privately owned house or apartment. For a cohabiting or married couple it is likely to be built around two incomes, as many women now are in some form of paid employment. There may or may not be children, but there will be fewer of them per household than a generation ago, and far fewer than a hundred years ago. Almost everyone will expect there to be at least one two-week holiday every year, probably abroad in Spain or some other hot country, and many will be used to more than one foreign holiday a year. A modern lifestyle will probably involve a good deal of eating out, from a meal with the kids at McDonalds to Sunday lunch in a country hotel. It will mean, for most, the income to buy clothes and electronic home entertainments of a kind and origin undreamt of not long ago. There will, perhaps surprisingly, be more do-it-yourself around the house and garden with the growth of leisure time and of the retail warehouses and garden centres that make it feasible. There will, perhaps, be less neighbour-liness than many adults remember from their youth, and more friendships at a distance due to personal and social mobility. There may, in retrospect and despite the plentiful goods to buy in the shops, be more unease and dissatisfaction with such a lifestyle than would have been so with the lifestyles of the past.

Clearly, these are caricatures into which bits of our lives and our thoughts fit better than others. But the descriptions will have meaning for many from the wealthier parts of the world, and some from what we may have assumed to be the less developed world – South Korea, Taiwan, Venezuela or Mexico, for example. Yet all the descriptions contain comparisons with the past. The pictures are snapshots of a moving scene. It was not always like this the commentary says, not yesterday and certainly not years before. How did the changing idea of what it is to be modern begin? Why do we now think the way we do about trying to be as modern as we can in our possessions, the fashions we follow, the places we visit? Why do we throw things away when they aren't broken or even if they are?

In the far distant past, peasants, for example, might expect to make one long journey in their lives, a pilgrimage to Santiago de Compostela, Rome, Jerusalem even, but otherwise stay fixed within a small geographical area, within walking distance of a town, or maybe not even that. Only an ecological disaster such as famine or a social one such as war could force a change to a settlement pattern established over generations of attachment to the land. Change would occur, but slowly, faces would be familiar, today would be like yesterday except, as the seasons changed, working lives and social lives would mingle at various points of the year, at harvest obviously, but also at the sowing season. Then in the winter, with less to be done, social life would focus on the home, or tavern if there was one, and entertainments would be self-made, handed down or communal, historical, unconsciously understood expressions of tradition. The church and the simple class structure would bind the whole together into a system of unchanging ideas and practices, valued precisely because they were shared with friends but also, perhaps, social enemies of the present, as well as the past.

Modernity as emancipation and anxiety

Modernity, if it exists, is clearly much more than one-dimensional. It is therefore a most elusive idea, one that invites the unwary to think of it as a totality, some set of thoughts and practices having enough in common over space and time to encourage us to generalize. Reflection gives us good reason to pause before assuming that because we have given some historical experiences, events and practices a common name we have thereby put the reality they may represent in a common box. In his recent writing on modernity Jürgen Habermas, a social philosopher, has traced the origins of the word back to at least medieval times where it was used, mostly in ecclesiastical circles, to refer to artistic novelty in forms of expression. In particular, it was used to contrast innovative representations of religious ideas or motifs with those of the ancient civilizations, especially of Greece and Rome.

By the time of the Renaissance, however, such medieval avant-gardism was being referred to as premodern. The reason for this was that the Renaissance represented a rediscovery through detailed scholarship of the methods, techniques, literature and art of the ancient world itself. The Renaissance was reflective regarding the aesthetic and philosophical principles on which the ancients based their culture. Moreover, it was a period in which those principles were reworked in new ways in painting, writing, architecture and so on, such that the innovations of the medieval period were considered archaic. As a result it was this rehabilitated classicism, especially as represented in ancient Greek culture, that was now to be described as modern. Even in its origins, therefore, the idea of modernity was paradoxical, recursive, linked but not bound to a particular time period or temporality.

From the sixteenth to the eighteenth centuries what it was to be modern continued to exercise the minds of contemporary intellectuals. Roger Bacon used the term 'modern' to refer, possibly for the first time, to the new ways of thinking and acting that became possible as other fruits of the Renaissance, science and technology, began to bear upon culture and society. Later there was raging debate – 'The

Battle of the Books' – as intellectuals and ecclesiasts wrangled over whether the products of the seventeenth century modernity of their times were of comparable or inferior cultural and aesthetic quality to those of the ancient world. But by the eighteenth century, punctuated with the philosophical Enlightenment, the elevation of human reason to a privileged position in western thought, and the occurrence of the French Revolution as a partial consequence, modernity was being thought of in terms more recognizable to ourselves. Reason could be used to make the future a malleable one, and could interrupt the flow of history, overturn traditional hegemonies. Modernity was now to be understood as the very expression of individual and collective reason to bring about the achievement of some great social project. Thus emancipation of the individual, social progress, the development of harmonious social relations, the overthrow of fixed social institutions from the church to the calendar – Year One the revolutionaries called that following their overthrow of the old order – became the victorious definition of the idea of modernity. To a large extent, the past was to be relinquished, even forgotten as individuals and societies stepped into an unknown, unbound and therefore potentially terrifying future.

It is in this general sense that the idea, practices and experience of modernity have come down to us. These are closer to the understanding of the French revolutionaries, with a strong injection of Bacon's technological or inventive modernity, than to that of the medieval or even, perhaps, the Renaissance perspective.

Charles Baudelaire, writing in the 1850s, gave slightly more definition to an individual, subjective dimension of modernity that had been overshadowed by the collective, social connotations prevalent earlier. Baudelaire wrote about the experience of being a post-Revolutionary, also post-counter-revolutionary Parisian. As Marshall Berman has so brilliantly shown, Baudelaire momentarily pinned down the new experience of being part of the crowd in the newly constructed boulevards and arcades of Paris. It was an experience that was to be repeated in the lives of millions of immigrants forced from the land or towns by famine, disaster, pogrom or simply agricultural modernization. Prussian peasants going to live in Berlin, Russian peasants moving to St Petersburg, or Irish peasants emigrating to New York would share Baudelaire's feeling about modern life, experienced in the streets as transitory, fugitive, contingent.

Modernity was experienced as transitory because it meant personal and social upheaval from the settled peasant existence of agricultural life. Thus family members would be separated as the male headed for the city in one of the migration streams in pursuit of work. When he arrived he might or might not find familiar friends to take him in, but if he did it would not be for long. He would move from rooming house to rooming house as he moved from factory to workshop in quest of work. He might become an itinerant, falling back on some locally learned skill as a survival strategy in what could often seem to be a hostile, transitory, urban world.

The fugitive quality of modern urban life was a product of the fleeting nature of social interaction. Since practically everyone in the streets or cafes was a stranger, conversation, were it to take place, would inevitably be qualitatively different from that in the home town or village. It would be superficial, perhaps exploratory, and there would be a search for common ground, but also a fascination with widely divergent personal histories and narratives. There could be little sharing of assumptions, plenty of room for misunderstandings. Chance meetings could sometimes result in feelings of friendship or intimacy developing as two or more people discovered common interests. But then, the chance encounter would come to an end and the participants would possibly never again see each other. There might be a period of searching but also the dawning of recognition that modern life entailed the conscious or unconscious possibility of hiding from too much emotional exposure. It is little wonder that the less existentially minded migrants would huddle in ethnic enclaves in the modern city. Nor is it surprising that existentialism as a philosophy of action (and inaction) should thrive in Paris, as it had earlier in the literature of St Petersburg where Dostoevsky worked out his terrifying, emancipatory fantasies.

Modern experience also has a contingent quality about it. The nominally free subject, the conscious individual, can choose a course rather than experiencing life as a series of necessities. Different occupations can be sought and relinquished rather than being determined by the requirements of the land, the seasons, the duties of settled existence. Circles of acquaintances can be extended, assignations made, and satisfactions purchased in a contingent way, dependent to some extent on mood, opportunity and availability. Long-established practices, such as the rituals of religion and culture, can be shirked. The modern person finds herself in Paris and learns French; in New York, English. She lives in a world peopled largely of her own choice, she develops habits, but also breaks them. She falls back on her own resources, particularly reason or maybe just common sense. She has a benchmark of comparison with her former life, learns to be critical, notices differences, aims to improve. It is as a consequence of these experiences that the modern individual both forges herself but is also forged by the contingencies of everyday life.

It is, then, this transformative quality that characterizes modernity so precisely: the idea of life as an adventure of self-transformation within a looser set of limitations than those familiar to the past, the possibility of life being perceived as a project over which the individual has considerable influence, though not total control, is what specifies modern experience.

However, the question of modernity is neither simply one of existential joy nor is it purely a subjective experience. Projects go wrong, and relinquishing the familiar can lead to 'fear and loathing in Las Vegas' as Hunter S. Thompson puts it. Upward mobility can reverse as the contingencies of private enterprise eject, having previously welcomed, the new employee. For this is also a central part of modernity. The individual who becomes an entrepreneur in a system which rewards the competitor or the innovator excessively is engaged in adventures with far-reaching consequences. Modernity as conceived here coincides with the onset of competitive capitalism. That system of production requires the unshackling of egotistic urges, insists upon the harnessing of individual and collective reason in pursuit of success in the competitive marketplace.

Markets and the new productive system, which must expand to survive, exert social pressures not unlike the physical forces of an electro-magnetic field. They penetrate outwards, weakening towards the edge, but disrupting the social spaces, towns, cities, regions with which they come into contact. The agricultural region from which the nineteenth century Parisian modern(e) might have migrated would have had markets of course, but small local systems of exchange. Competition from a region in which modern practices of investment, improvement and technological development were prevalent would bring about two crucial effects.

First, it would force those in the less developed region to adopt, by purchase, some of its practices and products. But these would not be exchanged equally. Capitalist production embodies the element of profit. To exchange products across the regional market boundary requires the payment of that profit element by the producers of the backward region. This gradually sucks capital which otherwise might have been stored in local banks, ready for investment in that region's own modernization, away and into those of the advancing region. This unequal exchange of value lies at the heart of the market system.

But, secondly, and more importantly, the advanced productive system, which will most likely be more specialised, concentrating on a smaller range of products to increase the advantages of economies of scale, will outcompete in price the more hand-raised products elsewhere. Specialization will be augmented by a more efficient division of labour amongst the workforce. The way in which the labour force is organized will also be a source of profit to the entrepreneur. This is because, although paid a wage, this will not fully compensate them for the value of their daily or weekly effort. It will be sufficient for them to live but not equivalent to the worth of the work completed. The backward peasantry will in fact, and temporarily, be wealthier than the hired labour of capitalist agriculture and related industries such as food-processing, canning and so on. In time though, that advantage in scale will undermine the capacity of the peasantry to produce even for their local markets at competitive prices. Farms will be sold, the younger generation will increasingly see fewer prospects of employment by staying, and some of them will become the modern inhabitants of the cities which now, through their concentrations of factories, will have become the labour markets of the future.

The aesthetics of modernism

The social forces unleashed by such development processes created tensions outside the spheres of everyday and employee life. The 'shock of the new', as Robert Hughes has put it, does not simply wash over the modern citizen, leaving only surface traces on a passive sensibility, it is actively created and recreated by individuals and groups who experience and reinterpret it. This is especially pronounced in the sphere of aesthetics where ideas, innovations and cultural transformations are projected from thought into practice more rapidly than the changes going on in society, politics and the economy. The question of aesthetic modernism is a difficult one. There is debate about when it really got started, whether it can be thought of as a homogeneous phenomenon, and what its key characteristics might be.

Regarding these three questions, it is simplest to deal with the first one, though in so doing an argument has to be made to justify what some writers would see as an arbitrary cut-off point. For present purposes a date around the mid-point of the nineteenth century can be proposed. Developments in the arts, literature, music and so on having connections with the cultural forms of the first half of the nineteenth century and before can be referred to as proto-modern. Thereafter, it is convenient to speak of early modernism taking us up to the turn of the century, a middle period from then to the mid-twentieth century, and late modernism being associated with the period from 1950 to the present.

The reason for choosing the mid-point of the nineteenth century to start the discussion and definition of the modernist aesthetic era is because that was when the contours of aesthetic modernism became clarified, first, as a discipline which united artists against the past, and, second, as the spirit of what they were setting out to express and achieve. It is undoubtedly true, that some outlines of modernism can be detected before this time in literature more than perhaps art or music. Romanticism, as in the writing of Goethe, contained fundamentally modernist elements in the concept of man 'binding himself while binding back the sea'. There is reference to the Prometheus myth which emphasizes the poignancy of his punishment – being chained to a mountainside and daily eaten alive – for defying Zeus by giving the gift of fire, and thereby enlightenment, to humanity. One could say that Shelley, for example, defined his literary and political life in Promethean, and hence both ancient and modern, terms; so, it is fairly apparent to see, did Byron in his epic poetry on the life paths of modernist figures such as Don Juan or the equally autobiographical Childe Harold. Byron of course, even more than Shelley, was personally committed to assisting the Greeks in their quest to form a modern nation-state by overthrowing the Ottoman Empire in their country.

Despite these motifs, conjoining Enlightenment ideas of personal and political freedom, it cannot be said that these writers posed a fundamental challenge to the cultural norms they had inherited. To some extent the political activity of Byron and Shelley was a displacement of that challenge from the cultural sphere to the world of action, a world of action beyond their own native borders. For Wordsworth, too, political radicalism, galvanized by the French Revolution, turned into an introspective communing with nature, and the aesthetic experience of its religious power and beauty. Indeed this could be said to be the defining characteristic of Romantic proto-modernism, a pessimism turned inwards into an aesthetic code of regret at loss of innocence in the face of experience. Shelley's 'Ozymandias' is an expression of the futility of the works of man in the face of the twin forces of nature and time. Wordsworth turns back to reflect on the simplicity and harmony with nature of the life of the humble leech gatherer; while Keats, the other great Romantic poet of the proto-modernist period, sought solace in the timeless aesthetics of classical figurative art in his ode to a Grecian urn.

If Romantic proto-modernism is ultimately aesthetically conservative what is it that gives modernism a more radical, emancipatory temper? It is, if anything, a turning away from tradition that defines modernism. Whereas Romanticism ended up in celebrating the past, aesthetic modernism made a break from it and celebrated the future. But the break was not a complete one, since links were retained with classicism. In architecture even the most cube-like constructions such as those designed by Mies van der Rohe or Le Corbusier employed the harmonious mathematics of the 'golden section' discovered by the Greeks. In painting, figurative representation remained the major motif, even for experimental modernists such as Picasso or Matisse. And in the novel, the narrative tradition strengthened so that even in Joyce's masterwork, often taken as the exemplar of modern-

11

ist writing, there is structure, movement, development. Significantly, he called it *Ulysses* and its hero Dedalus.

Nevertheless, that link was everywhere stressed and strained in reinterpretations and new forms of expression as artists experimented both within and against the inheritance of the past. The idea of progress, projected most pervasively during the French Revolution and by the Enlightenment thinking that informed it, was a crucial stimulus. Moreover, the conditions of existence in which artists and writers lived and worked influenced what they sought to represent. The world was changing rapidly, and large cities had grown with the industrial revolution and the development of the empires. New inventions, technologies, labour processes, methods of transport, and styles of life surrounded and infused modernist aesthetic sensibility. Thus a novelist such as Dickens flooded his narratives with critical observations of the workings of the competitive capitalist economy of his day. In *Bleak House*, possibly his greatest novel, the machinations of the legal system are anatomized; businesses and the people running them are represented. Unlike earlier work such as that of Jane Austen, Dickens was not concerned to dissect the manners of domestic bourgeois life nor, as in the dramas of Racine or Molière, project upper-class manners and forms of speech onto classical or contemporary figures. Dickens represented urban social and economic life as he saw it, with a sceptical eye, a concern for the casualties of what he saw as a heartless system, and an underlying belief that things could be different and better for more people than they were. Of course, Dickens could write beautifully of the natural world as his descriptions of the fens in *Great Expectations* or the fog on the Thames in *Bleak House* testify. But, unlike some of his writing about characters, especially women, which was often too steeped in sentimentality, these scenes are realistic evocations of nature acting naturally, as it were, not supernaturally as it can often seem to be in Wordsworth. So modernism in Dickens, and also in George Eliot and even Thackeray, but

categorically not in Scott, is increasingly realist not romanti-
cist.

But it is to France that we look for the fullest unfolding of
modernism proper. Modernism depended on developing its
own aesthetic *avant-garde*. Charles Baudelaire represented an
archetypal figure of the Parisian modernist vanguard, as did
Flaubert, though much of his time was spent outside Paris,
working in Rouen. Baudelaire captured the sense of crises,
personal and social, that the experience of *modernité*, the
term he invented, gave to aesthetic as well as wider aspects
of consciousness. His characterization of that experience as
transitory, fugitive and contingent captured the new sense
of time and space associated with modernity. Paris itself
with its modern boulevards, created a new sense of urban
space, aesthetically informed, a deliberate stage-set as well
as parts of a functioning city. This sense of space or
spatiality in the modern urban environment was provided
by a focusing of city morphology onto centralized features
such as monuments or grand public buildings. Movement
through the city was not any longer a question of winding
through a medieval maze of narrow streets and back alleys;
rather the modern street structure encouraged the taking of
a particular route to a specific destination. This funnelled
crowds onto the primary boulevards, and gave a sense of
random encounters with large numbers of unknown – yet in
ways such as dress, appearance, speech – familiar people.
This opening out of space, echoed also in the creation of
large squares or circles which could also enclose it in
structured ways led to a compression of time or temporality.
People, and most particularly vehicles – first horse-drawn,
later motor-driven – could move more quickly, dodging in
and out of the crowds and traffic. Meetings might be brief,
and dangers lurked for the unwary as traffic hustled by the
packed pavements. A certain amount of psychological
adjustment had to be made, a degree of pre-planning, of
anticipation, of preparedness both to cope with the urban
dangers but also to enjoy the urban spectacle. The personal-

Figure 2 The definitive dandy.

ization of modernist aesthetics occurred in the forms of the dandified *flâneur*, the street character darting in and out of the crowds, showing off, dressed-up, perhaps sauntering down one of the new arcades walking a turtle on a leash. Or the *boulevardier*, strolling arm in arm with his ladies, dressed to the nines and heading for the theatre, restaurant or opera.

Baudelaire; Flaubert and others wrote about the new experiences of aesthetic consumption to be derived from gazing into the arcade shops, admiring the new public architecture and the avenues or parks that Baron Haussmann had laid out, partly for military reasons, partly for display. This aesthetic freedom was also an aesthetics of rebellion. The vanguard, introducing the new, whether in fashion, painting or literature, was in revolt against the past, against the stifling rules of tradition. To be new, to think new, to admire newness was the fate of the modernist mind. Therefore what was new today would also be challenged by tomorrow's innovation. Style and fashion could be expected to be fleeting.

In the quest for the new, wild outgrowths of the old could be explored in decadence, in outrageous behaviour, in shocking the sensibilities of normal society, whether in the academies or at large. But hedonistic expressions of emancipation could also be moderated by the hard labour of aesthetic exploration. Thus the artistic movement that came to be called impressionism arose from the attempt by Monet and others to capture the fleeting experiences of natural phenomena, most notably light, on canvas. This art was representational but seeking to convey sense-experiences in new, less precise forms than classical, traditional representational painting had done. The shock of the new to the guardians of aesthetic judgement was such as to cause the impressionists to rebel against the official *Salon* society and establish their own *Salon des Refusées* to exhibit their work.

Post-impressionism, as represented in the painting of Cézanne, for example, explored the nature of reality informed by a consciousness of the solid geometry of things. Cézanne believed that phenomena depicted in painting could best be represented by deriving them from geometrical forms such as the cylinder, cone or cube. Of course, Picasso and Braque took those discoveries to their hermetic limits in their radical development of Cézanne's ideas in Cubism. And so, the *avant-garde* differentiated as it developed.

Most of it was considered to be outrageous by the old guard, receiving, even celebrating, names such as Fauvism, the art of wild beasts, given to one particular movement. Movements came into existence not only in France, but in other countries, seeking new forms of representation and later non-representation in the simple abstractions of colour. Surrealism sought, in some ways, to shatter the illusions surrounding commodity-driven society by juxtaposing contradictory forms in an art which often celebrated uselessness but also exposed the psychological tensions inherent in modernity. Moreover, and especially in the work of Magritte, the aim was to show that painting could not be representational but rather only presentational of itself. Magritte's famous painting of a smoking pipe entitled 'Ceci n'est pas une pipe' speaks for the break which modernism now had made with the representational art of the past.

In music, the atonality of Webern, Schoenberg and Stravinsky broke with the accepted parameters of classical harmony, conveying in Stravinsky certainly, not the pastoral beauties of a season, as in 'The Rites of Spring', but the wild, almost barbaric expressions of awakening, growth, dynamism and sexuality, with rhythms drawn, as the Cubists had done, from Africa or from jazz, to provide a sense of the inner meaning of sprouting renewal.

Thus we see in the aesthetics of modernism both a limited degree of continuity with the classical past, and an increasing opposition and rebelliousness towards its norms. We see a willingness to explore beyond the limits of representation, a new and quickened sense of temporality and a broadened but structured sense of spatiality. However, in some ways much of the modernist aesthetic sense was a secret one shared only by an elite for whom its originality gave to it and them a specific aura of exclusivity.

The modern nation-state

As well as witnessing the overturning of classical aesthetic sensibility the nineteenth century also saw the birth of the modern nation-state and the party system which sustains it. The pre-modern nation-state is a contradiction in terms, although prefigurative examples can be found. Perhaps pre-modern England, France and Spain are the nearest equivalents except that they were more understandable as early and absolutist states rather than nations. The question of nationality in the modern sense scarcely arose although issues of power, organization and, above all, territorial expansion clearly did. One especially interesting feature of the pre-modern state that contrasts markedly with modern nation-states is that there was relatively little concern displayed regarding the national, cultural identity of those who comprised it. Pre-modern states were dynastic entities within which diverse cultures co-existed, adhering to dissimilar religions and speaking numerous languages.

Because the peoples who were the subjects of these dynasties had only limited rights which could be ignored by those in power if necessity dictated, and which certainly did not extend to political rights as we would now understand them, they were fundamentally excluded from membership of the territorial system in which they found themselves. They were ultimately its subjects and as such were affected, often in a negative, controlling way, by its laws. But in other respects they might have limited freedoms which we do not have today. Though most people would not, as peasants, move very far from the piece of land to which they continued to be tied under the feudal system through their life cycle, it was possible for them as individuals and groups to make extremely long journeys on some occasions in their lives. These journeys would not be particularly hindered by the existence of territorial boundaries in the way that an equivalent modern journey would be. Pre-modern political space was relatively open compared to that of today. Thus pilgrims could go on their lengthy journeys without particular fear of political harrassment, although banditry could pose other kinds of problem. The concept of the mercenary was certainly one which was well understood and quite widely practised across dynastic boundaries. And for those subjects involved in a trade, enjoying the status of freeman or some equivalent, the idea of journeying from one end of Europe to the other to ply that trade was, if not normal, then not by any means unthinkable. Hence, within particular structures of accepted validity – religion, war, trade – mobility could go relatively unhindered.

Of course, there were limits. Thus the Christian pilgrim would at various times be prevented, by the threat of extinction, from paying homage at the very source of his or her religious belief if and when the territorial expansion of Islam redefined the greater boundary of Christendom. Then, in some sense, that boundary became one between space and non-space. The latter, the territory of the barbarian or the infidel would be a space into which the believer would not go, unless it was as a soldier on one of the Crusades to re-establish the geographical links with the Christian shrines. But that the Crusades were fought precisely to enable believers to pay personal homage is testimony to the importance attached to geographical accessibility across imposed boundaries.

Religious struggles remained central to the formation of the early versions of the nation-state. The expulsion of the Moors from Spain was predicated on the successful military organization of the powerful regional state of Castille, a vehicle which then turned northward and westward to fight battles against other unbelievers, whether Protestants as in the Low Countries and England or the sun worshippers of the Americas. But economic questions were becoming significantly intertwined with such expansion. Wars had to be financed, colonies appropriated, and competitors, especially for maritime ascendancy, controlled or defeated. Thus territorial aggrandisement became both an expression and a provocation to emergent national sentiment. National identity was still closely bound up with the question of religious affiliation but religious domination was itself becoming increasingly an economic issue.

In the Low Countries, for example, the early success of Flemish producers in the woollen cloth industry and their associated wealth, fine architecture and art was not only an economic provocation but one which later became a focus for religious and political strife. Moreover, it was based on trade, first with the North Sea and Baltic countries, later across the Atlantic. The Catholic south with its adherence to the continental system sought to control the open-trading policies of the Protestant north. Thus, as in England, the threat to economic freedom combined with the struggle for religious freedom and contributed to the development of national identity. Once successful trading rights had been established, backed by the ensemble of an organized religious, political and military machinery, then, as in the case of Spain earlier and in England and the Netherlands later, territorial expansion on a global scale became feasible.

But if a recognizable prototype of the modern nation-state had emerged in some countries before the nineteenth century much of Europe still remained medieval and feudal in its political organization. In Germany, Italy and eastern Europe there were empires, kingdoms, duchies, counties and city-states. Some of the latter were successful mercantile powers in their own right – Venice, Genoa and the cities of the Hanse in the Baltic – but clearly not nation-states. By the second half of the nineteenth century such micro-powers had developed, but they were clearly suffering from the subsequent rise to greater economic power of those older proto-nation-states, and pressure to absorb them into coherent, competitor states with homogeneous and centralized territorial control became imperative.

The processes of modern nation-state formation are interesting for their similarity at the large scale, with the experience of modernity at the scale of the individual and of the development of modernist aesthetic sensibility. For modern national movements were and have to some extent continued to be Janus-faced, as has been suggested by Tom Nairn and others. That double profile involves a process of social innovation in which tradition is reappropriated to seek the unification of diverse strata within and across a defined territory and to mobilize a society to support the move forward into an unknown future. The quest for modern nationhood normally involved the resurrection of what can be termed the folk culture of the dispossessed as well as the reinterpretation of the heroic acts of past military leaders, particularly where the latter involved some successful rebellion against an alien hegemony, or better still the creation of a glorious, though now lost, empire. Past and future were thus synthesized in the ideas which contributed to the *invention* of the nation.

This raises the vexed question of whether or not the modern nation-state owes its origin to fundamentally economic or politico-cultural rationales. There is agreement among many thinkers on the essentially economic reasons underlying the formation of nation-states. These are often argued still to underpin the rise of neo-national movements such as those in Scotland, Wales, Brittany or the Basque country in the contemporary era. Thus Tom Nairn, from a leftwing perspective, sees the expansion of the nation-state to encompass greater colonial territory as a necessary function to secure the expanding market for the sale of the products of industrial capitalism. From a more conservative position Ernest Gellner conceives of nation-building through the establishment of common educational standards, a dominant language and a homogeneous culture as necessities to the modernization of a country through industrialization. It is, of course, difficult to argue that economic innovations are absent from the rhetoric and practices of national movements. The burden of the preceding argument also rests to some extent upon this assumption.

However, it is instructive to note that the forces directly responsible for nation-building are seldom industrialists or bankers but often monarchs, politicians (of course), bureaucrats, philosophers, poets, historians and others involved in what can be called cultural production. There is clearly some important non-economic motivation underlying national movements and the origin of the modern nation-state. The reappropriation of the past, which is precisely the task of historians and other cultural gatekeepers, is essential to give definition to the idea of progress which governs the modern temperament. To know with any degree of certainty the nature of the social institutions which may be created or reinvented in the new nation-state, it is necessary to identify motifs from the past. These would ideally be distinctive to social and cultural groups present within the prefigurative national territory, and distinctive from those of outsider nations as well as from those of imperialist powers against which national struggles were to be waged. Such requirements gave rise to the need for synthesis, and the invention of traditions, as Eric Hobsbawm shows, which embodied diverse, culturally reproduced symbols. Thus the tartanry of Scotland, having been militarily repressed, was manufactured anew and absorbed into the military forces representing the new British nation-state after the Act of Union between England and Scotland. Later there were Irish, Scots and Welsh (but not specifically English) Guards to protect the Crown.

In other contexts, where a pervasively common culture was recovered, as in Germany or Italy, it was more a case of establishing definite state forms, through administrative, legal and military structures and ideologies harking back to the greater glories of Prussian or Roman traditions, to give distinction and cohesion to the modern nation-state.

Later, developments occurred in methods of political

representation as the struggle for internal dominance over those nation-state institutions produced political cleavage. Divisions often occurred on class lines, themselves resulting from economic modernity and the unleashing of industrial capitalism, but expressed politically through an increasingly democratized, inclusive nation-state. Inclusiveness was, by the late nineteenth and early twentieth centuries, a necessary corollary of the social mobilization inherent in the struggle for nation-statehood.

But in the process of homogenization through political, administrative and cultural centralism, the modern nation-state, always dependent upon the consent of its subjects, could overstep the boundaries of consent, provoking responses requiring coercion. Such backlashes could arise where what Nairn calls historic non-nation-states and their cultural gatekeepers in the arts, government and political life perceived the possibility of regional annihilation. Where this was linked to religious and economic discrimination and disadvantage, as happened classically in Ireland *vis à vis* the British nation-state, then the weapons of aesthetic modernism could play a part, as in the poetry of W. B. Yeats, for example, along with those of political and quasi-military resistance, in initiating another, later round of national struggle. This too would call on the past to deal with the dangers and opportunities of the future which pointed to the formation of a new and independent nation-state.

This, then, seems to be the one certainty when it comes to generalizing about the development of the nation-state. Individual as well as collective experiences and powers of mobilization are rooted in the concept of progress, itself perhaps the defining characteristic of modernity. But the perils as well as the emancipatory powers of progress demand the placing of one foot in a frequently prefabricated past in order to proceed into the uncharted territory of the future. The formation of nation-states is thus a profoundly modern subjective and collective experience.

The cities and regions of modernity

The pre-modern city was often a site of administration and consumption. The objects of administration and consumption were largely to be found in the countryside, the labour and production of the peasantry. The division between town and country where the inhabitants of the former were the exploiters of the latter was the kind of class-based division that so exercised modern critics of the origins of capitalist development, most notably Marx. Relationships which could appear timeless where rulers lived lives of varying degrees of luxury while the ruled laboured to produce the food and clothing necessary for the survival of both, persisted in some otherwise modernizing nation-states even into the twentieth century. The *latifundia* of southern Europe was a system of social relations which for cultural and political as well as economic reasons was self-reproducing, but it ultimately dug its own grave. The system, with variations partly determined by climate and geography, had much in common with the feudalism of northern Europe and produced a degree of homogeneity over space that was consonant with the relatively unbounded nature of pre-modern political geography.

The local aristocracy in concert with the church, its ideological support and dependant, expropriated rent from the peasantry in exchange for their right to work the land. The peasantry though, not owning the land on which the crops and stock it laboured to raise were produced, nevertheless owned the means of production, the tools, implements and skills necessary to the process. The peasantry was, to that extent, freer in the production process than the factory worker, though in other respects, such as the freedom to sell its labour on the market, it was less so. There was, nevertheless, an element of double dependency in the relationship of peasantry to landlord. Neither could exist without the other, a relationship which gave rise to certain customs, practices and informal rights respected by both parties. Even Marx commented, not wholly unfavourably, on some of the benefits of stability and security in both economic and social relationships which such a system provided, though he condemned what he saw as the 'rural idiocy' which it also fostered. This 'rural idiocy' was later anatomised, in the Italian context, by Antonio Gramsci, jailed for his Communism by Mussolini. Gramsci showed how within this system even the cleverest son of the peasantry had only the most limited of escape routes from a life of interminable agricultural toil. Through the monastic system the church offered one local escape route everywhere; the local professions of notary or minor administration offered others. Each of these branches also acted as the prop of the system of exploitation; thus the peasantry could never develop its own 'organic intellectuals', and would always be re-routed back into a position of supporting the status quo. Hence the persistence of the division, which was also a class division, between town and country. The aristocracy – rural landowners but also urban residents of palatial mansions – controlled Gramsci's 'cities of silence' from which little protest was to be heard.

Only where agriculture had become modernized, capital-ized and geared to production for the wider market, was the formation of a class of agricultural proletarians, no longer masters of their own means of production, possible. Where this occurred, as in parts of northern Italy and more pervasively in northern Europe, rural labourers, with only the chains of wage slavery to lose, could and did form solidaristic syndicates or prefigurative trades unions to struggle for improvements in wages and conditions. More-over the beginnings of production for the market meant also the growth of mercantile capitalism and trade which, either through the primitive factory system or more generally by means of *métayage* or the putting-out system, helped to loosen the feudal bindings on the freedom of labour. Towns and cities were where the freedom to sell labour to the highest bidder could be expressed. They were either the final or the intermediate market for industrially produced goods.

Hence, the modern city was increasingly a site of production, though it was also one of administration, capital circulation (through the banks, merchant houses and residential landlords) and consumption. Textile production was often responsible for the growth of modern industrial cities in the nineteenth century, as it had been in less fully urbanized settings such as Flanders, eastern England and parts of southern Europe a century or more before. The development of capitalist agriculture, 'improvements' to the land which included the enclosure of the commons, and rising rural population partly contingent upon such improvements forced migration from the countryside to towns and cities. The growing availability of urban labour power further stimulated merchant capitalists to invest in factory methods of production and technology. The industrial city rapidly became an emblem of modernity and economic power to be emulated in the late-comer countries possessing the resources and aspirations to compete in the developing system.

Housing and work developed side by side, magnifying, though dividing, the relationship found in the domestic industry of the putting out system. In industrial cities the demand for factory labour dictated a close proximity between work space and living space. In the absence of developed public transport services the journey to work was often on foot, or later by bicycle. The modern industrial city was, nevertheless, made and remade according to the social conditions prevailing at any given time. Initially, such cities as Manchester (see Plate 1), Bilbao, Copenhagen or Turin consisted of a mixed, somewhat chaotic, overlay of medieval street patterns and buildings, new factory buildings and housing both for the wealthy and the poor, the latter crammed into tenements or terraces squeezed into the former gardens of grander houses, or along the main transport routes such as rivers and highways. But the

25

modern temper was formed by a concept of progress, a belief in the capacity of social forces to make significant changes to inherited conditions, and a belief in the possibility and necessity of social order.

Thus, it was in the modern industrial cities with their confused urban fabric, polluted air and water, and teeming slums, that political consciousness both on the part of the new industrial bourgeoisie and the urban working classes whom they feared took its most progressive form. The idea of progress was the grand narrative that provided the motivation for the transformation of cities. This narrative was expressed in the desire to organize, control and give a central focus to the unstructured and dangerous urban mass that was forming. This purposiveness could be seen in the emergence of municipal authority, the clearing and reconstructing of the overcrowded core of the city, the construction of grand public buildings such as the city hall, law courts and cultural facilities – museums, opera houses and theatres – often set in an imposing piazza, the whole sometimes modelled in a reworking of Renaissance styles. Crumbling slum areas would be cleared, forcing the poorest urban dwellers further to overcrowd the newer but poorly built tenements. The impact of Baron Haussmann's grand plan, realized in Paris, pervaded the thoughts of progressive urban reformers in many other countries, though few could emulate what he had achieved. But in these new city plans, the expression of authority was frequently frozen in the new architectural forms.

A strong sense of the need to distance the urban poor from the dwelling spaces of the affluent was provoked in the fear engendered by the masses. Outbursts of social conflict and rioting by the working-classes, often caused by the cyclical nature of early competitive capitalism which could deprive them of wages without warning, added to the fear of contagious diseases which poverty brought in its train and led quickly to the segregation of space. The forces of authority, represented in public buildings, often funded at

26

least in part by private wealth, controlled the centre of the modern city. Their luxurious shopping and entertainment facilities structured and separated the centre from the slums. The rich would occupy segments of space, controlled by the rental value of the land, and push outwards in a quadrant away from the dirt and disease of the working class areas, along the improved roads on which their horse-drawn, later motorised, vehicles would carry them.

The modern grand narrative of progress with its subtexts of centring, segregating, distancing and thereby reorganizing the space of the city into an authoritative social order reached its peak with the development of railways and related modes of transportation. Where Haussmann had driven boulevards through medieval Paris, the railway companies drove their routes through the slum quarters surrounding the city centre. In virtually all modernizing industrial cities these enterprises reorganized urban space in definitive ways. They also created the means of maximizing distance, segregation and the centre–periphery structure of the city by means of suburbanization.

Escaping the congestion and pollution of the city now became a possibility both for the rich and, more slowly, the poor, for industry as well as commerce. Suburbanization started in London in the second half of the nineteenth century. Many railway companies developed branch lines to link distant villages and empty green fields to the great termini in the heart of the city. The speculative developers followed suit by building villas and houses in the style which had come to express the aesthetic revulsion of the middle classes for the raucous contingencies of modern urban life, garden-city suburbia. The English attachment to a bastardized version of Ebenezer Howard's idea of a self-sustaining community set in a green backcloth became the dominant residential style for the upwardly and outwardly mobile. It crossed the Atlantic and had an even stronger impact on city life and city structure in North America. Modernity now meant accessibility to urban workspace and

27

culture but also escape from it into a synthesized version of an imagined rural, cottage-like lifestyle. Suburbia with its Janus-face is quintessentially modern.

The spread of modern cities into the countryside along the railway and, later, highway routes was also a necessity for working-class housing. Many of London's working-class areas expanded eastwards and southwards along the new transport routes once pressure had been put on the railway companies through Parliament to introduce cheap workers' fares. This housing, still exclusively privately built, was often poor in quality and quickly became multi-occupied, but much of it is still to be seen adjacent to the railways as the traveller cuts through the urban class structure from north, east and south. Such areas became the newer municipalities and boroughs with their own distinct administration and political culture. Industry also migrated outwards from such cities to take advantage of particular pools of labour, notably married women. The modern city was, in some cases, becoming a city region.

Transportation links, technological developments and local resource exploitation often brought a wide-ranging interaction between modern industrial cities and their regional hinterlands. The specialisms of the cities became specialisms of ever-increasing elaboration projected on to the wider regional space. Regions became important economic entities not focused particularly upon the national capital city but on the regionally dominant city. Manchester was the exchange and production centre for a wide-ranging network of subsidiary centres of specialist cotton-textile production linked through trade to the world markets. New competitors would spin off from established companies and establish bases in smaller centres within the regional system. The industrialization and urbanization processes would then be repeated, sometimes on a more planned scale, as at Preston, Charles Dickens' Coketown. This pattern was repeated throughout Britain, Europe and the USA.

But the peak of the modernist period either side of the

Second World War saw the beginnings of the erosion of such specificities. The loss of regional ownership through capital concentration and monopoly, rises in living standards and the growth of mass markets led to, first, the delocalization of large-scale production units to the suburbs and beyond, later the rapid loss of population, factories, commerce and, of course, jobs to the sometimes semi-rural settings of the urban fringe, and later still the globalization of location as new markets and production centres in other continents and less developed countries were established. The late modernist city was either an increasingly deindustrializing hulk or its central spaces had increasingly been devoted to the towers of an inaccessible financial industry, attracted to the core principally for high rental values.

CHAPTER TWO

Community: the social residue of modernity

Modernity versus community

Many of the best-known social commentators and theorists of the nineteenth century were stimulated into action in large part by the changes they could see proceeding in the world around them. This is not unusual, but the mid-nineteenth century was exceptional in that change on an epochal scale seemed to be pervasive. To get a grasp on the nature of some of the social effects of these changes contrasts were made between the features that characterized the recent past, and could still be observed outside the centres of urban modernity, and those that seemed to denote the future of a society dominated increasingly by industrial capitalism. The very origins of an academic discipline such as sociology, and, it may be suggested, many if not all of the wider social sciences, can be traced to the reception by social observers of the onset of modernity.

The fascinating problem that exercised many of them, most notably social theorists such as Emile Durkheim, Karl Marx and Max Weber, was how was society possible? How, given the disruptive changes, the uprooting of peoples, the development of new ways of living and producing, and, above all, the projection into economic and social life of the competitive ethic, did society remain orderly, at least in the sense that it did not, apparently, break down into Hobbes' 'war of all against all'? In partial answer to that huge

question social analysts began anatomizing the ties that
bound individuals, families and social groups together and
contrasted those mechanisms of cohesiveness with whatever,
different or similar, mechanisms they could identify in the
modern, usually urban, setting where development was
most strongly pronounced.

In thinking about the differences between the different
kinds of social order that could be envisaged and observed
such writers and their successors often placed great weight
upon the concept of 'community'. Not all of them were
users of the concept, but many had a reasonably clear
picture of what had typified social relations in the pre-
modern period and what was being replaced under the
power of modernity. Community was contrasted with
association, first in the work of Ferdinand Tönnies; for
Durkheim the differences lay in different kinds of social
solidarity, traditional societies displayed mechanical solidarity, modern ones organic solidarity; Weber conceived a
pervasive trend towards what he called rationalization, an
increased administrative, rule-governed way of organizing
social relations, often associated with a growth in bureaucracy, underpinned by the state's monopoly over coercive
power. This he contrasted with older modes of social
cohesiveness rooted in religious or military qualities of
leadership which could be termed charismatic. Rules,
present in some form in all societies, were nevertheless tacit,
or understood without having to be spelled out.

Weber's distinctions were comparable though not identical
to those of Durkheim. Mechanical solidarity was simply
received by the individual subject through processes of
socialization in the family and wider society. Everyday
practices were routine, persons defined themselves in terms
of group membership of an almost unconscious kind.
Individuals were ascribed roles and, in the main, they
complied with them. In the city, though, as we have seen,
such rules and roles had to be discovered. Social relationships were more negotiated, expectations of solidarity could

not be assumed but had to be forged, possibly in the workplace. Such associational links with others, shallower than those of unreflective, traditional life, had to be nurtured, fostered, almost fertilized in a more organic way. Interestingly, neither Durkheim nor Weber, nor indeed many of these social commentators, Marx included, emphasized the positive aspects of organic solidarity or association upon the individual or the creation of new kinds of community, to any great extent. Unlike their literary colleagues who, as we have seen, were fascinated by the emacipatory power of modernity, these writers took a gloomy view of the transition to modern, industrial capitalist society.

The latter phraseology is more that of Marx than of the more mainstream thinkers of the time, though Weber was happy to talk about the rise of capitalism as a distinctive form of production for the market. Marx thought on the grandest scale. For him the contrast was not with a past of traditional stasis, rather he saw capitalism, and the social relations on class conflict and exploitation on which it was based, as a revolutionary overthrow of the decaying, feudalist mode of production. Exploitation of ruled by rulers characterized all modes of production other than primitive communism for Marx. But capitalism represented the highest form of exploitation. He, too, contrasted it, at least in terms of the psychology of the individual worker, in negative terms. Such social relations and the labour processes necessary to produce things with exchange value on the market was an *alienating* experience. It dehumanized mankind when persons were treated as things to be bought and sold in the labour market while things could be fetishized as desirable commodities. Like Durkheim, who developed the similar idea of *anomie* to describe the psychology of the lonely figure who cannot integrate into organic solidarity, and whose last recourse might well be suicide, this new society was often to be contrasted unfavourably with the communal and community life of the past because of its immiserating capacities.

For Weber modern society appeared as an iron cage of rule-governed behaviour. He too took the gloomy view of the effects of Enlightenment thinking and practices upon the social individual. He foresaw the coming of mass-society in which only the few, and they not necessarily elected, would do the thinking, would determine the values that were to drive on the projects of modernity, and the rest of society would be reduced to dull conformity. This kind of thinking became widespread in other continental countries, notably Italy, where writers like Michels and Pareto also perceived the 'iron law of oligarchy' as the necessary corollary of not only modern society but of all societies. Such thinking was, of course, consistent with prefigurative political forms of authoritarian rule, and the later depredations of Fascism and Nazism. Weber never went that far, but others in their gloom at the prospect of developed modernity, Nietzsche particularly, seemed to yearn for the restoration of charismatic leadership as the expression of a nihilistic will to power. Ironically, these political ideologies also projected a romanticized image of community, of attachment to the soil and to the family, back on to the peoples they were to lead into the cul-de-sac of history.

Community as culture

What *was* that community being blown away by the advent of modernity? Much of the effort of modern sociology was to be centred upon that question. Had it, in fact, been so obliterated? Could communities be identified in modern contexts? A discourse of 'community studies' developed first and most extensively in France, particularly following the methodology of the French engineer Frédéric Le Play. This remarkable man devoted half his life to the study of communities all over Europe. Three dimensions of analysis informed his studies: folk, work and place. The combination of the natural setting in which peoples existed, the resources which they found available to them to mould into the materials necessary for life, and the kind of settlement pattern these practices gave rise to made up the element of place in the analysis. The organization of the processes of appropriating nature, the kind of agricultural or industrial activity that dominated particular places, mining, fishing, pastoral or arable farming and so on, varied from place to place. Thus work gave further definition to the practices of distinctive social groups. In some settings, as in the vineyards of southern France, some parts of the work of wine production would be organized around the family as the basic work unit, other parts such as the processing of grapes into wine would be organized co-operatively amongst the villagers. Elsewhere, work would be more individually organized, as for example in upland livestock rearing or certain craft-related activities. In mining or metal-processing work would be collectively but not co-operatively organized under conditions of private enterprise, and so on.

So the folk element of the equation was to a large extent conditioned by environment and the kind of work it made possible. But the folk also brought variable norms to these conditions. The key distinction between primogeniture and partible inheritance would mean that the way communities developed in similar environmental conditions would vary. Partible inheritance meant a denser settlement pattern, primogeniture forced siblings away from the family on maturity. The combinations of such cultural values, centred upon the family but shared amongst a particular social group and environmental context where work was the major organizing focus, gave communities their particular local distinctiveness, but also their similarity to other communities in distant lands of which they could have no knowledge.

These ideas had a remarkable influence upon the early British school of civics sociologists, amongst whom was the leading urban planner of his day, Patrick Geddes. He, like many modern urban reformers at the end of the nineteenth century such as Ebenezer Howard, Raymond Unwin and

others, sought to modify the still haphazard proces
urbanization then in full flood in industrialized societ
Geddes thought that the problems of modern social life,
anomie, social dislocation, suicide – he was influenced by
Durkheim and had heard him speak in London – arose from
the separation of folk, work and place that were entailed in
capitalist development. The uprooting of peoples, their
immigration to the towns, separation from families, involvement in apparently meaningless, abstract labour needed to
be controlled, even reversed. Instead of these revolutionary
changes to social life, the development process should, he
argued, be evolutionary, planned on a city–regional scale so
as to have a less disruptive effect upon social life. Urban life
should seek to be organically whole, should be constructed
around the concept of community and should place human
values above economic ones.

Such ideas became remarkably influential as the twentieth
century progressed. They chimed with other rejections of
naked modernity as in the guild socialism of William Morris
and John Ruskin. They became an important strand in
British socialist thinking and received their fullest material
expression in the postwar urban planning policies of
restricting metropolitan growth by means of a Green Belt,
and channelling surplus population into satellite New
Towns constructed on principles of neighbourhood communities. The belief was that such principles could break
down the class-structure and the resulting social segregation
typical of modern cities. People from different occupational
and income backgrounds would co-exist, use the same
amenities, send their children to the same schools. As a
result a more egalitarian, organic social model would be
formed. Its success would perhaps in time be emulated
elsewhere, even in the divided cities. Not surprisingly these
ideals were never fulfilled in reality, the classes mixed very
little, the professionals and employers sought and found
exclusive residential enclaves, social divisiveness proved to
be a far stronger social motivation than the desire for the

and values of community life.

new communities had been led astray
community studies. It is now clear that
of these studies had examined were
ms. Scanning collections of these studies
;ether by Ronald Frankenberg it is striking
e communities under inspection are rural,
remote from the mainstream of modern life, or small-scale,
semi-industrial occupational communities inhabiting the
geographical and functional margins. The classic studies are
of communities on Gaelic-speaking islands off the west coast
of Ireland, the Welsh-speaking heartland of Wales, or the
marginal industrial settlements of West Cumbria. To be
sure, studies of community life in urban settings can also be
found, such as those of Bethnal Green in London or Hunslet
in Leeds, but they too seem residual, on the verge of
extinction, transforming as the younger generation moves
outwards and upwards in the social hierarchy.

This notion of community as residual culture developed
from the ideas of Raymond Williams on the processes of
cultural production and reproduction. His analysis, unlike
that of many sociologists, especially those influenced by a
mixture of Durkheim and Weber, stresses practices rather
than values and norms. His is a materialist rather than an
idealist analysis. This means that instead of seeing culture as
tending to be imprinted upon people who are compliant
receivers of processes of socialization through the family and
the education system, he sees it as being created and
recreated by the conscious practices of individuals and social
groups. Williams contrasted residual culture with what he
called culture in dominance, *dominant* culture on the one
hand, and *emergent* culture on the other.

The dominant culture has, since the mid-nineteenth
century, become modernity and, as the great social theorists
of the nineteenth century recognized, modernity is associational rather than communitarian. Modernity is founded on
a scepticism of the stability, rootedness, respect for tradi-

tional, collectively transmitted local norms and values typical of rural, agricultural, marginal society. As we have seen, modernity is steeped in the idea of progress, change, challenge to though not total rejection of the past, self-emancipation, social reform, inter-generational improvement and material well-being. Modernity is captured most accurately in the suburbia to which the offspring of Bethnal Green's residents aspired, and indeed migrated. In early modernity this was the emergent culture. By the 1960s it had become the dominant culture, widely available to the mass of working people, many of whom were enjoying affluent lifestyles, experiencing *embourgeoisement*, becoming middle-class in their ability to afford consumer goods and foreign holidays and to buy their home.

In the process, communities, especially those studied by the community studies researchers, were often already quaint in their adherence to family, kinship and communitarian values. This lack of desire to change (for those who were modern were not there to be interviewed) suggested a passive, though strong, consciousness and valuation of traditional norms regarding religion, and loyalty to established institutions whether local, such as the pigeon club, or national, such as the monarchy (one Welsh study focused largely on the activities of the carnival committee in coronation year 1953). When, as Ray Pahl found, these cultures clashed as they were increasingly seen to do in the new commuter villages of the Home Counties, the community divided around the control of the local cultural institutions. The newcomers tended to take over the Women's Institute, the more attractive of the pubs, the running of the school. The residual culture seldom fought back to regain control of these institutions; its practitioners melted into the back bar, organizing their traditional events separately, and maybe eventually moved away as rents rose.

But what of industrial communities? Were these not newly created in the process of modern industrialization? Attention focused for a time on what were called 'occupa-

tional communities', places where working lives were
shared, income levels were similar, people lived inter-
generationally in the same working-class housing (it is
difficult to find studies of middle-class occupational communities; the idea itself seems almost a contradiction in
terms, though studies of white-collar workers in the
workplace are to be found) and seemed to subscribe to
communitarian norms. Mineworkers, saltworkers, quarry-
men and fishermen (for these were not women's labour
markets) comprised such occupational communities. Some
could be conceived as being emblematic of modern industrial
society, though there is a distinct ambivalence in that most
such occupations clearly predate modernity also. Textile
workers in the factory towns of northern England are a
better case. The problem with such material is that it
inevitably focuses more upon the culture of work than the
interaction between work and everyday life. Sometimes it
showns how work culture, for example where an employer
adopts a paternalist style of management, providing workers
with certain leisure or welfare amenities but in exchange
refusing trades union representation, and managing the firm
almost as an enlarged family, has carried over certain values
such as deference into everyday life so that workers in such
settings habitually vote against the election candidate who
represents their interests. More recent comparative studies
of such occupational communities show that work culture in
historically similar settings could give rise to different social
and political outcomes where work was organized in
distinctive ways. Occasionally, as in the case where women
workers were allowed to take supervising instead of the
more normal operator grades of work, some of them might
carry the confidence gained from responsibility in the
workplace into local political and community life, becoming
local activists and pressing, for example, for improved local
welfare services.

Often the high point of working-class culture in occupational communities was passed once the institutions of late

modernity got a grip on them. Amongst the most corrosive of these institutions have been the emergence of the centralized welfare state with its distanced provision of universal standards and administration in the areas of health care, social benefits and education; state ownership and control of some of the industries which gave definition to such communities, notably the coal and steel industries; widening accessibility to the means of mass consumerism through the medium of advertising, availability of consumer credit, and the concentration of ownership in retailing; and the spread of the various forms of mass culture through films, television, centralized newspapers and the rise of consumer sociability centred on drinking and club or pub-centred leisure and entertainment activities. The secularization of culture, the tendency for market relations based on exchange to replace church- or chapel-centred and home-focused socializing, with pub life a male preserve, to some degree an extension in a more convivial setting of relationships originating in the workplace, unravelled important elements of community texture.

Raymond Williams, in his search for a new basis in late modernity for a revived community life, tended to overlook these problems. He wrote of the coalfield of South Wales:

> into which in the nineteenth century there was massive and diverse immigration, but in which, after two generations, there were some of the most remarkably solid and mutually loyal communities of which we have record. These are the real grounds of hope. It is by working and living together, with some real place and common interest to identify with, and as free as may be from external ideological definitions, whether divisive or universalist, that real social identities are formed. (Williams 1983, p.196).

It is true that such communities were not only passive receivers of inherited traditions of mutual assistance rooted in a farming culture of rural turbulence, opposition, and the struggle for democratic control, but they also reinterpreted such history in the new, urban context. This was done, first, through the nonconformist chapels, later through the trades unions and their offshoots in the political and educational clubs, friendly societies which enabled, for example, house ownership to become widespread, and the local health and welfare services which were paid for by community-controlled deductions from wage packets. Community was, in this case, modern, collectively emancipatory, politically reformist, as to some extent it had been even in a deprived agricultural setting. There was little deference or passivity to be found in such contexts. Here a modern culture of active community, consciously reproducing itself in modern ways, and seeking to influence the wider, dominant culture by social and political example was in being. Up to the point, that is, where it was overwhelmed by its own success.

The modern welfare state, the modernizing nationalized industries and the spread of a culture of affluence and consolation deprived such communities of the social energy which they had generated in forming and maintaining their own institutions. The modern nation-state, infused with a centralist vision of progress, loosened the ties between work and home by rationalizing inefficient coalmines and steelmills, replacing them with factory employment located at a distance from the mining towns. The gradual, then accelerating, pace of deindustrialization created a spiral of poverty, marginalization and recourse to basic survival strategies. The break-up rather than the reinforcement of family life has been a consequence of the intersection of motifs of mass culture and the activities of the modern nation-state. It could not have been otherwise; modernity invades and transforms culture, leaving only the residue of vital community life as its agent, industrial capitalism, moves locust-like over space finding, then deserting, locations where it has gained temporary refreshment on its long circulation of the modern world.

Community as power

Is there no defence against these upheavals, the transformations of self and society which modernity, the institutional
application of reason in pursuit of progress, entails?
Throughout the modern era, the major source of possible
defence against the destructive effects of modernity has
been the modern nation-state itself. True to its Janus-face
the same institution has often been instrumental in enforcing
or enabling the weakening of those defences. But for the
moment let us examine the state in its more protective
disposition. In particular, attention can be drawn to the
universal presence in modern societies of the local or
municipal part of the state's apparatus, that part charged
with the function of representing and meeting, as far as
possible, identified community needs and aspirations.

In the pre-modern era local government existed but was
variably organized over space. For example, in some towns
it was effectively in the hands of the vestry, the committee
of local church- or chapel-connected members who could
discharge numerous functions from appointing local constables to providing poor relief. Elsewhere, there might be
the remnant of some feudal institution such as the court leet
with its symbolic head the port reeve undertaking local
administrative tasks. In most cases such institutions were
under the control of the local ruling class, but with the onset
of early industrial capitalism the highly localized manner of
industrialization could mean that control would fall to local
sympathisers with the radical cause. As Gwyn Williams has
shown for Merthyr Tydfil in Wales, and John Foster for
Oldham in northern England in the 1830s, the vestries were
able to make important decisions favouring the interests of
local communities driven to despair or to proto-revolutionary
activity by the wild fluctuations in markets, hence wages,
under conditions of harsh competition. These decisions
could range from appointing constables known to be

41

sympathetic to the workers' cause and therefore unwilling, for example, to evict them from houses for which they could not afford the rent, to making generous, even debt-incurring allocations of poor relief to the starving unemployed. The emergence of such forms of community power hastened the great reforms of the early nineteenth century, including the reform and modernization of local government itself.

Well into the twentieth century there was remarkably wide responsibility for discharging responsibilities at local level. The modernized form of poor relief, unemployment benefit, which though means-tested was still locally controlled in the 1930s, is a case in point. And new rights were being added, such as those to build housing for rent and implement local development schemes without recourse to central adjudication. Levels of expenditure were simply dependent on the amount of rates income that could be politically sustained, and in strongly Labour-controlled communities relatively astronomical local expenditures were registered on local services such as education. Much of the income for such expenditure was derived from business and industry, poorly represented in such local authorities, while domestic rates based on rental values were generally extremely low. Hence, for many decades limited social improvement could be sustained in the absence of central interference.

However, over time, and accelerating during the period of late modernity after the 1940s, more and more of the determining powers over community expenditure were removed from local to central state level. This was particularly so once the welfare state with its universal norms of provision was established. Moreover, the nationalization of utilities removed control of the provision of services such as gas, electricity and, subsequently, water from local control. The relationship between the nation-state and local government changed from something of a hands-off one to one in which the local level increasingly became a conduit for centrally determined decisions on levels of expenditure for

services such as housing and education. That this te
was not confined to Britain is evident from the situatio
for example, the Scandinavian countries where income tax
paid in varying degrees to the municipality which, however,
increasingly spends that income in terms decreed by the
central state. Moreover, there is a strict division of functions
for which Nordic municipalities are responsible. They are,
for example, constitutionally prevented from assisting
industry directly by making grants or loans available to new
or existing businesses, though they are expected to make
infrastructural investment which will inevitably assist
industry as well as the community. On the other hand, in a
country like Denmark virtually all social welfare expenditure
is undertaken by municipalities as the central state withdraws
from direct responsibility in that area.

With the local level of the state in many modern societies
having retained important powers and gained some others
by the 1960s, more and more investigative interest was
being shown in the questions of who exactly ruled decision-
making at community level, and of how community power
was controlled. These questions were first asked of American
communities where local government enjoyed considerable
autonomy and relatively little federal subsidy to pursue its
policies. As early as the 1930s studies of community power
structures began to show that there were ruling elites who
formed networks of influence and information controlling
the local decision-making process. A number of other
studies in the 1950s tended to confirm the impression that
when, for example, it came to the question of whether or
not land should be rezoned to enable suburbanization to
occur, or who was going to be appointed to the various
administrative boards responsible for managing day-to-day
affairs, the same 'local mafia' was involved directly or
indirectly in determining outcomes for the community.

By the 1960s, though, a counterview had developed.
Examining similar decision procedures in a wide range of
cities on issues such as urban renewal and the location of

tional facilities, many political scientists
politicians or 'local notables' were
decisions. Also, it was shown that the
ner by the threat of voting for the
xt election or by organizing in pressure
influence decisions affecting the com-
ork soon gave rise to a critical backlash.
nonious and pluralist democratic process
the critics ce... l that, under the surface, there was a
mobilization of bias which favoured decisions serving the
interests of the local bureaucracy, which in turn served
those of the power elite. This modern conspiracy theory
strongly suggested that communities were relatively power-
less and subject to manipulation in a system where they
were sometimes thrown an apparent, though in reality
unimportant, victory to sustain the pluralistic myth of
community power.

In Britain there was a considerable effort, stimulated by
the American findings, to find out the extent to which the
community decision process was in any way similar to either
the more democratic or the more oligarchic power structures.
The answer seemed to lie somewhere between the two but
with a bias towards the oligarchic. Local mafias and political
caucuses tended to be commonly identifiable, though the
system was occasionally open to community protest against,
for example, road-building plans or urban renewal schemes
provided such participation was carried out in an orderly
fashion. Also it was found that the multitude of community
associations found in most areas were sometimes represented
in limited ways on council sub-committees where they had a
voice but not a great amount of influence on crucial issues.
Community representatives could, therefore, be active in a
defensive posture, but even then their victories were few
and far between.

The 1960s were, in many countries, years of growing
concern and involvement by community groups faced with
the rampant development and redevelopment of the urban

(and rural) fabric. Numerous researchers of a radical political persuasion were influenced by the studies of French urban protest which culminated in the events in Paris of May 1968 when it appeared that a popular alliance of community groups, students and workers might even topple the government of General de Gaulle. One of the leading writers on those events, Manuel Castells, claimed to have identified a new, powerful form of community participation which he named the 'urban social movement'. The interesting aspect of the political conflicts in which such movements became involved is that they were often stimulated by the urban restructuring and community dislocation caused by modernist planning and architectural design. Older areas of cheap housing where distinctive occupational or ethnic communities had found shelter were being demolished to allow new roads to be built, or retail and office developments to be established. New high-rise dwelling complexes were being constructed on the outskirts of cities where there were few amenities and little opportunity for retaining community links, something not of course confined to France. And on some occasions community groups took to the streets, put up barricades, or marched on city halls. The prospects of such groups joining force with the wider working-class movement protesting about pay and working conditions seemed to pose a serious threat to the projects of modernity in the urban setting. However, little actually changed.

The urban revolution against the modernization plans of the western nation-states petered out. Even Castells recognized the overoptimism of his analysis when, in a later book which examined urban social movements in different countries and at different times, he redefined such movements as having a variety of bases other than class, and as cultural more than political. They were now to be understood as autonomous sources of community effort to redefine the image or meaning of their urban territory. Urban social movements exist to challenge and change the meaning attached to particular areas of cities in the minds of the ruling elite. Such efforts would include trying to change the city council's perception of a slum area ripe for redevelopment into one which recognized the historical, social and cultural distinctiveness of the district. If successful, then more sensitive (even aesthetically and ethnically conscious) local policies could be implemented to conserve and improve the area in question. The protection and marketing of 'Chinatown' in contemporary cities is a case in point. Thus, a local coalition of diverse interests consisting of heritage, environmental, minority and developmental plurality might all have their demands satisfied. Here, perhaps, were the origins of a new, issue-based form of community politics, one of alliances and partnerships.

This was an extremely important insight because it signalled a recognition on the part of the centralist, distanced agents of modernity within the state apparatus and the development and finance industries that the motifs of architectural modernism were becoming exhausted. Many cities in most of the modern, advanced economies began to develop policies to refurbish old, declining areas of cities, not just residential but industrial or warehousing zones too. London's Covent Garden was saved from demolition, unlike its parallel, Les Halles in Paris, which was transformed into a modernist hyperspace of shopping malls, rapid transit links and urban spectacle. While London retained its politically progressive local council in the early 1980s it was even possible to some extent to retain the community flavour of a long-established working- and middle-class mixed neighbourhood such as Covent Garden. Thus the freeholds of shops and dwelling blocks were acquired by the council, enabling rents to be kept low. Low-rent housing was refurbished making it possible for poorer residents to remain. But of course the working base in the fruit and vegetable markets had gone and soon, as in many such exercises in the architecture of *la mode retro*, rents began to rise as the rich began to move in.

This process of urban displacement, the winkling out

even in the most unpromising areas such as derelict docklands of the remnants of urban communities, has occurred wherever the critique of modernism has taken root. Baltimore Harbour, Boston's Faneuil Hall, San Francisco's Fisherman's Wharf, Vancouver's Gastown and Granville Island, and the London Docklands, many of them preserved from demolition by community action, have turned into luxury playgrounds for tourists and urban pioneers. Accordingly, and sadly, even the limited exercise of community power has, in many cases, turned into a whirlwind of 'retro' modernity and blown community away.

Community as justice

As we saw in the discussion of the character of the modern nation-state its typical form is a sovereign institution, the repository of legitimate authority and power, comprising citizens who both recognize those disciplines but are also constitutionally entitled to legal rights of protection against the exercise of its arbitrary powers. The habits, customs and norms of community in its pre-modern sense seem opposed to this impersonal, ordering device. There is then a real tension in this relationship, or perhaps non-relationship as some would see it. Tönnies, one of the earlier analysts of this tension, sought to draw together some of the oppositions between community and the individualism of association which he had, after all, polarized by the use of idealized, oppositional categories. He proposed that, in practical terms, the pure oppositions could never be found. Rather, real societies consisted of a mixture of community and association, with the former often present as at least a noble ideal and the latter enhancing, through its objective, civilizing and universalizing character, the cultural basis for the realization of the ideal. Tönnies' somewhat utopian solution to the tension was to propose an 'associational union' as the ideal form of the sovereign nation-state, a union of all the associations, a harmonious forerunner of the model of the pluralist community based on legalized rules of citizenship containing a concept of both rights and duties.

For less conservative observers of the modern nation-state such as Marx and Engels such legal niceties as abstract equality and individual autonomy acted to disguise the manifest inequalities and compulsions present in economic relations. The idea and institutionalization of rights and duties would be replaced by the principle of 'from each according to their abilities, to each according to their needs' in the legal order of communism. The latter would also, it was proposed, see the withering away of the state as a consequence. These arrangements would be the community of all communities. Thus, the materialist analysis was fundamentally rooted in the idea of an irreconcilable opposition between communality and citizenship on the terms of the modern nation-state.

In commenting on more recent attempts within juris-prudence to reconcile this tension Timothy O'Hagan has argued that many thinkers have sought to show that there is no necessary incompatibility between community and the idea of sovereign individuals of the state. The positions outlined range from conservative to liberal and radical. They are often constructed on modern interpretations of the insights of the ancient philosophers Aristotle and Plato, and rereadings of such insights by early commentators on the nature of modernity such as Hegel and Weber. Aristotle, for example, conceived of community as social sharing, its highest form to be found in the city, where man, the fundamentally political, not solitary, animal engaged in civic communication in the pursuit of personal character develop-ment and social virtue. Recognizing the distinctiveness of this moral sphere from the particularistic sphere of private, commercial transactions, he nevertheless thought that natural law could accommodate both provided the superiority of the first over the second was recognized.

For Hegel, it was the linking of law with morality that gave definition to modernity. The development through history of the concept of freedom as individual and institutional rights, especially in the example of social contracts which formalized property rights as personal but also alienable, was a cornerstone of modern morality. Such achievements as the realization of freedom in the communal institutions of modern society were what set the epoch apart from its predecessors. As we have seen, Marx, Hegel's philosophical capsizer, saw this evolution of institutionalized freedom as the simple legitimation of self-interest. And Weber too, though for different reasons, disagreed with Hegel's thesis. Modernity had seen the increasing separation of legal from religious norms, and in the process a gap of widening proportions had opened up between law and ethics. The law had become a set of rational procedures, professionally controlled and interpreted, benefiting those with the technical expertise to apply it.

Weber's despised, professionally closed circuit of inter- pretative experts finds modern defenders amongst conservat- ive thinkers who can, as in the case of Lord Denning, react strongly against the impersonality of constitutionalism and celebrate the organic growth of *ad hoc* judgements by his peers under the common law, itself idealized as the expressive will of the community, More cerebral thinkers such as Ronald Dworkin have been criticized for a different – though related – kind of conservatism. Developing the modernist idea that the judge rather than the legislator is important (rather as some literary commentators see the critic not the author as crucial, since it is the criticism of texts rather than their creation which improves standards) he advocates the legal community as the only true safeguard of a just society. Their shared value system enables them to advance the key individual and communal right to equal concern and respect and to marginalize claims to privilege for other rights. The idea of the legal community as a coherent, ethically united body is considered somewhat overoptimistic by *his* critics.

The liberal position is represented best in John Rawls'

theory of justice. This is founded on the idea of community as the well-ordered society. Two basic principles of justice regulate this imaginary community. The first is that each citizen has access to a range of basic rights. Examples would include the right to life, knowledge, leisure, religion, sociability, aesthetic experience and so on. These rights would be compatible with the rights of all other citizens within the community. The second principle is that social inequalities can only be justified *either* if they arise from appointments or positions for which there is equality of opportunity, *or* if their existence maximizes benefit to the least advantaged citizens. Thus, a higher salary than average could be justified for doctors or surgeons since there is a limit on their numbers and they aim to heal those with a particular health disadvantage. However, the first principle takes priority over the second, basic rights being the cornerstone of the just society.

The problem with Rawls' theory is that it is difficult to see how such a community would integrate citizens pursuing their own scheme of rights into a consensus willingly and freely entered into. In responding to this criticism Rawls retreated into the sort of socio-psychological theorizing that Dworkin was also prone to. The motivation to fit into community norms would come through socialisation of the citizen by the family instructing the child in the social virtues of communality. The result would be a social consensus for this scheme of justice. The incompatibility between the modernist right of individual freedom to pursue projects and the possible consequence of doing so by paying low wages to the socially disadvantaged to make such a life possible lies at the heart of the Rawlsian dilemma. There is, furthermore, always the possibility of there being a consensus amongst the citizenry in favour of social injustice. The contradictions in the liberal theory of justice testify to the difficulty, if not impossibility, of grafting an anti-modernist concept of community on to the modernist concept of individual liberty and rights.

Recognizing the probable futility of such schemes, the radical position advocated an approach which was rights-centred but attacked the authority of the legal community to be the authoritative interpreters of the law. This approach was one which sought to undermine the grand narrative of the rule of law and to develop a responsive form of law based on the pragmatism of social advocacy and community politics. The development of pluralistic, local narratives would have the effect, it was thought, of diluting the idea of sovereignty, leading to the withering away of the state. The result would be a devolved, pluralistic community life. The heroic optimism of such a position, neglectful of the power asymmetries of modern society, has given way latterly to what has been termed the romantic pessimism of the vision of a post-modernist community.

In the work of Roberto Unger the premise is a rejection of the anti-modernist fantasy of the integrated community with its supposed coherence, absence of conflict, acceptance of authority and centrality of the family. Unger reworked Tönnies' dichotomy between 'association' – characterized by particularism, competition, impersonal rights, separation between public and private life, where the law enforces utility and security – and 'community' – universalist, authoritative, customary, public–private mixed, where the law enforces the virtuous life. Modernity indeed has two principles of justice, argues Unger, and they can be boiled down to, first, freedom of contract, which serves the money-making ethic, and, second, a counter-principle of community, which attempts to prevent or regulate the pervasion of all walks of life by the first principle. This idea connects with one of Jurgen Habermas' major theses, namely that modernity uncouples the systemic elements of history – the social system, the economy and the state (the repositories of money and power) – from what he calls the 'lifeworld', the spheres of culture, community and personality. The problem of modernity is that these systems, rule-governed, formalized and structured by principles of rational calculation, expand their influence to produce a 'colonisation of the lifeworld'. For Unger, community has actively to be formed and fought for rather than inherited, to prevent this tendency. Nor does he accept the relativist anarchy that was built into the radical critique of liberal theories of justice. Rather he sees community as a zone of vulnerability, the weaknesses of which may be mitigated by the trust built up through pragmatic discussion between persons passionately committed to the struggle for egalitarianism and the pursuit of personal and social power.

So, to some extent, the discussion of community as justice has come full-circle but moved on to a higher plane. The central opposition between community and individual freedom noted at the outset of modernity still structures the development of the most contemporary thought. But the difference, giving to contemporary thought its possibly post-modern flavour, is the idea that community has actively and consciously to be created anew in defence of a sphere vulnerable to colonization by the morality of the marketplace. Critics of Unger's view comment on his pessimism, his improper opposition of the two principles of modernity, and his belief in the impotence of modern society to achieve consensus. But as we have seen the burden of modernity points in favour of his perspective.

Community as history

Modernity reveres the future yet it also venerates the past. But just as modernity can be conceived as giving rise to the separation of the systemic sphere from that of the lifeworld, it also separated them both from the aesthetic sphere. The modern era gave rise to the culture of the museum, the art gallery, the exhibition. The past could be objectified when presented as a finished project, and the establishment of the ubiquitous museums of *modern* art signified the break within aesthetics *per se*. The museum developed as a repository of the finest achievements of the past, especially the ancient past of Egypt, Greece and Rome. It was expected that the sensibilities being appealed to by such exhibitions would be those of the educated bourgeoisie, and it made sense to think that only such strata would have a consciousness of their own historicity; to the masses such experiences would make little sense. For them, the condescending aesthetics of mass culture were perceived as adequate. The important thing for the high-culture institutions was to maintain aesthetic distance from those of mass or low culture.

Hence, anything to do with the ordinary, the routine of life and its artefacts was excluded from the museum, except insofar as such objects shed light on primitive conditions of existence in ancient or prehistoric times. In much the same way history itself presented modernity as the achievement of leaders, elites and ruling groups and even when extended beyond the texts into the buildings it was castles and stately homes, palaces and baronial mansions that were to become the vehicle by which such preservationist organizations as the National Trust represented the achievements of the culture.

Robert Hewison argues that such institutional philosophies rest on a perception that:

> the heritage is something that is *under threat*. The threat is multiple: there is decay, the great fear of a nation that feels itself in decline; there is development, the great fear of a nation that cannot cope with change; there is foreign depredation, the great fear of a nation that is losing works of art it acquired from other nations in the past to economically more powerful nations like the United States and Japan. (Hewison 1987, p.137).

This narrative of decline is presently a powerful one, not only in Britain, but also in the United States of America, and much of contemporary politics revolves around the rhetoric and reality of its arrest. That this experience is becoming generalized within the culture is testified by one of the remarkable phenomena of late modernity, the aestheticization of everyday life, particularly the aestheticization of the everyday community life of the past.

Initially, the aestheticization of the ordinary past concentrated on the industrial processes of proto-modernity, such as the ironworks of Coalbrookdale or Robert Owen's textile mill at New Lanark; these superseded the tendency to objectify technologies by putting them in a museum away from their social context. So to turn the abstract experience of observation into the more aesthetic one of immediate involvement the industrial archaeological spectacle was born. But latterly, in what can only be described as a surge of industrial necrophilia, whole 'communities', complete with factory, mine and period actors playing the part of Victorian workers and their families in the houses of the period, have burst upon the scene.

In the USA, the equivalent, the predecessor in fact, is the Western theme park – Old Tombstone or Old Tucson – where you pass through the turnstile into a stage set which is, in 'reality' a simulation, a 'simulacrum', as Jean Baudrillard calls it. There are the sandy streets, the arcaded sidewalks, real cactus (for this is, after all, Arizona), adobe houses, bars and canteens into which you can walk and examine the dusty patina of the artefacts, and, if you time it right, a gunfight will take place in the street between you and the railroad depot, the iron way of which is just sufficient to house the wood-burning locomotive of a thousand cowboy movies. A living community has been recreated, but it is not reality, it is hyper-reality. There is no litter (or dead bodies) on the streets, the store signs are faded not with age but with special airbrush effects, there are no families, the only children are tourists, the artefacts are only occasionally authentic. Old Tucson is, indeed, a stage set, and was created by and for the film industry. Its most prized icons are the footprints and names of the stars who have trodden its boardwalks as actors.

Just as Old Tucson is more 'real' (yet wholly simulated)

54

than the original, so Beamish in northern England, a 'living' museum of nineteenth-century industrial and domestic life, is wholly fabricated from the remnants of early modern industrial society. Its shops, houses and means of transport are recreations of an imagined community in which one can talk to simulated Victorians speaking 'authentically' about their lives. Even more sober institutions such as the Welsh Folk Museum at St Fagan's near Cardiff has now installed a row of ironworker's cottages brought from the coalfield to arcadia in the Vale of Glamorgan to complement the more austere agricultural houses and artefacts which used to be its main symbolic representation of the folk history of Wales. Such centres attract tourists in their hundreds of thousands. What is being shown? What do we see? An imaginary journey, really into the inside of the images of nostalgia portrayed on television? Or perhaps a benchmark to compare our present position in society with that from which we or our forebearers originated? Or yet again it could be the desire at least to see, if not fully experience, something of the imaginary and perhaps real community life that the modern era first reshaped and then dispensed with.

Time-tourism of the ordinary kind reveals the ending of that distance which high culture sought to maintain from low culture. The gap is being closed as community and popular life, never fully colonized by the rational systems, science and aesthetics of modernity until its later phases, now themselves become antique. Museums of all kinds are now amongst the most popular of all tourist destinations. From Beaubourg in Paris, which some cultural commentators see as having been stormed and taken over by the masses, to Old Tucson and Beamish, not to mention Disneyworld, which are themselves sometimes the subject of eloquent discourses by cultural specialists, the aestheticization of the everyday life of the present and the past at a marketable value seems to point to a failure of modernity to preserve its separate identity. Culture has been democratized, even turned into a policy of 'community' revival for some derelict

Figure 3 The aestheticization of everyday life.

areas of the inner cities. As museum directors now contemplate selling their least popular exhibits to make way for spectacular mega-exhibitions we are witnessing the commodification of modernity itself.

CHAPTER THREE

Modern times: the Fordist worker

From craftsmanship to scientific management

An advanced stage in the preservation and likely commodification of industrial modernity was reached with the
announcement that one of the earliest European examples of
the flow-line assembly plant, the original Fiat motor works
at Lingotto in Turin, long abandoned with the expansion of
a new plant at Mirafiori, would not be demolished but kept
as a possible museum or cultural complex. The multi-storey
factory building required the production process to be
organized vertically. Raw materials entered the building at
ground-floor level, and the various stages towards completion
then took place on successively higher floors. On the roof of
the factory is the race track where the completed vehicles
were tested, and from where they were taken back through
the factory to be stockpiled and distributed. The Lingotto
factory (see Plate 2) was a modern anomaly, its organizational
principles American but its design European. Crammed into
its tiny urban location it was too linked to the past to be
truly functional.

Until factories such as Lingotto were built at the
beginning of the 1920s, during the middle period of
modernism, work had been organized on the shopfloor in a
very different way. Although American and European
industrial history differs in important ways, as do the
development profiles between European countries, one

generally common feature of the early modern period of development of the factory system was the retention of certain typically pre-modern community-based methods of organizing production. The skilled craft worker is centrally important to the story of early-modern industrial organization. From the era when 'free men' had established protective guilds in the towns and cities of medieval Europe, knowledge had been a protected commodity. For the skilled cabinet maker, gunsmith or producer of luxury goods, his craft was all that protected him from penury or a return to the relative powerlessness and poverty of rural life. Hence the guild system enabled craftworkers both to retain control over the secret knowledge they had developed, and to control recruitment and training of apprentices who studied at the feet of the master craftsman. Most importantly, craftworkers were in a position to bargain with the merchants and early industrialists who had the capital to expand production but not the necessary skills. Contract law enabled negotiated agreements between these parties to be reached. Craftsmen also made contracts with semi-skilled or unskilled workers they needed to employ. When a job was completed, contracts came to an end and contract workers were released, usually in the knowledge that they would be rehired for the next similar job negotiated by the craftsman.

This system persisted in the large-scale industries of the early-modern industrial revolution such as coalmining and ironmaking. But the contracting system was widespread through the advanced economies of the time. It varied in detail from region to region and from industry to industry but in essence control of the information, conceptual and practical, needed to produce commodities was in the minds and hands of workers, albeit privileged workers, rather than the owners of capital. The development of modern industry has, in large part, been the history of a struggle on the part of the owners of capital to wrest that 'know-how' away from the workers and to locate it within the managerial structure of the modern corporation.

The most incisive step in that direction was taken at the turn of the century when the industrial engineer Frederick Taylor began publicizing his ideas about scientific management of work. Scientific management meant turning the production process from an organic to a more mechanical, routinized series of tasks controlled by a central planning office. The office would then be responsible for the integration of tasks in the different stages of the production process. Each task would be submitted to minute examination, with 'time and motion' studies of workers' capacity to implement each task being carried out. Then each worker would be supervised closely to ensure that there was no backsliding. Hence, the conception and execution aspects of production would be separated, the 'skill' in the work process would no longer be in the hands and minds of workers. Ideally, Taylor advocated, workers should not even have to exercise conscious thought about improving task specification, they should simply accept orders from the technical experts, recognizing the limitations of their role as unskilled workers.

Not surprisingly, these ideas were resisted most strongly both by skilled workers, through their craft unions, and by management in companies nevertheless interested in cheapening the costs of labour by replacing skilled workers with unskilled ones. It was thought that implementing 'Taylorism' would require an inordinate number of unproductive technical and supervisory staff. Nevertheless, the context of production was changing, technologies which led to semi-automatic machinery were being developed, as was machinery to transfer finished sub-components at different stages of production. Some of these originated in industries such as lock- and gunmaking. Companies grew in size, especially in the USA, as competition led to takeover and mergers by the more successful companies, and markets became larger. These changes encouraged the adoption of Taylor's ideas.

In Europe, Germany and, to a lesser extent, France and

Italy first proved receptive to scientific management. It was not given serious consideration in Britain until the 1920s and 1930s and even then its spread was limited and tended to take place in newer industries, some of which were American and without a strong craft tradition. Craig Littler has pointed out that the adoption of scientific management by British firms was technically simpler because of the work of the Bedaux consultancy. Bedaux, an American firm, had taken Taylor's idealized techniques, simplifed them and made them more practical. Even in Britain, though, there was substantial opposition, more particularly from managers, who were not well-attuned to ideas of planned production methods. Workers, too, objected to time and motion studies and the personal surveillance they involved. The contract system remained in force in many older, established industries, notably coalmining and metal manufacture, though, even there, it was in decline as technological change rendered established skills increasingly redundant.

By the onset of the late modern period, in the years after the Second World War, traditional contracting relationships were scarcely to be seen in any major industry, although the concept of sub-contracting work out to external firms was a major feature of the British engineering industry. It was the old idea of the internal contract between the master craftsman and his employees, working as an industrial remnant of certain communal relationships of authority and dependence, even familial recruitment, that had – as elsewhere – disappeared from modern life.

Modernity and the development of Fordism

If Frederick Taylor had a hard time getting his ideas accepted in many companies, he had considerable success with the Ford Motor Corporation in Michigan. Mass production was not invented by Henry Ford; it had been present in other industries before he sought to exploit its potential. Michael Piore and Charles Sabel have pointed out that by the late nineteenth century the market for cigarettes could be saturated in the USA by just thirty automatic processing machines. Ford sought to create a market on a mass scale for a product, the motor car, that had hitherto been a luxury consumer item. The development of the Model T vehicle, embodying technological innovations such as the gearbox and clutch system, promised to be such a vehicle. It was reliable and easy to handle but needed to be cheapened in comparison to its competitors. Ford had noted how the unit costs of production came down as the volume of production increased, but he needed to find ways of reducing costs even further to create a market.

This was where Taylor's ideas helped significantly. By dividing up the labour process into small but repetitive tasks it was clear, as Adam Smith had shown more than a century earlier in his example of the pin factory, that the productivity of labour would increase dramatically. Smith, in *The Wealth of Nations*, had given the example of pin manufacture under craft-controlled production methods, and pin manufacture under industrialized methods with a division of labour. Craft production required that the individual worker undertook all stages of production from cutting wire to stamping, eyeing, sharpening, polishing and, finally, packing. Each task needed different skills. If the labour process was divided such that each individual task was repetitively undertaken by the same worker then that worker would become expert in completing that task correctly and, above all, speedily. So would the next worker down the line. As a consequence productivity would rise, unit labour costs would fall and the market could be expanded. Taylor's ideas were a detailed elaboration upon Smith's insight.

Taylor's contribution to Ford's intention was to show how this system could be set in place on a grand scale. The moving assembly line enabled workers to save time walking from place to place; the division of labour enabled each worker to become the swift executor of routine tasks. To complete the Fordist production system, two other technical requirements had to be satisfied. These, like Taylorism, required much experiment, trial and error before being perfected. The manufacturing technology needed to be as easily maintained as possible. This was extremely difficult due to the rigidity which production required; machines were dedicated to particular tasks, as were workers. However, Ford developed a system of interchangeable parts first for the tools of production and then for the product. The second technical requirement, to minimize the constraints imposed by technology, was to standardize the product, and this implied developing a sales force and a network of market outlets.

Apart from these difficult and innovative technical developments Ford also needed to secure two key social innovations. The pace and conditions of the Taylorized labour process created such pressure on individual workers that the turnover rate reached astronomical levels. To reduce the rate of labour turnover he instituted a sociological department, the tasks of which were to screen workers so that only the more docile, law-abiding and abstemious were appointed, and to look after the welfare of workers, including their domestic as well as workplace problems. For a time this forerunner of the modern personnel department was run by the distinctly disreputable Harry Bennett who, despite his underworld contacts, effectively ran the company during a short period towards the end of Henry Ford's life. Thus elements of coercion as well as consent were built into Fordist management–labour relations. Ford was virulently anti-union, for example, and Bennett's acquaintances assisted in preventing the signing of a union contract until 1941.

The second social innovation introduced by Ford, both to buy off the workforce but also, percipiently, to enable producers of his product to think seriously about also becoming its consumers, was to institute the five-dollar day. Five dollars was over twice the going rate for car assembly workers and it made the routinization of work sufficiently bearable for the relatively docile, nonunionized Ford workers for the system to work. As described, these innovations seem to represent the implementation of an almost sublime idea of a self-expanding productive system. It was not like that, and many of these innovations occurred in a piecemeal, costly and serendipitous manner. Nevertheless, by a mixture of chance and design, Ford had, by the outbreak of the First World War, mastered the methods of mass production that were to become the dominant feature of the economic growth process of the modern era. The mass market, once created, purchased the standardized Model T, available only in black paint, and heralded the onset of the mass-consumption ideology which became a key element of modernity. A central icon of modern times was the newly designed River Rouge car plant (see Plate 3) near Detroit where all the elements of Ford's production system were in place. Moreover, the production system was internally controlled from the first to last stages of production. As Piore and Sabel put it, 'iron ore and coal were fed into a steel mill at one end of this vast complex, and finished automobiles rolled out the other' (Piore & Sabel 1984, p.63). The giant production complex, vertically integrated throughout the various stages of production, capable of feeding a market of immense scale and giving employment to tens of thousands of workers had been set in place.

However, this impressive achievement was by no means the only model available for the modern industrial corporation. As we have seen, large-scale producers in Europe, somewhat later than in the USA, often retained a large range of small and medium-sized independent suppliers of both raw materials and components. Often this was partly a product of managerial conservatism as well as the relative strength, particularly of craft workers, in the older engineering industries, as in Britain and Germany. Even within the USA, Ford's main competitor, General Motors, followed a different developmental path. Instead of standardization, GM produced a product range for different segments up to the luxury end of the market. GM also retained a diversity of named companies within the corporation and provided the hire-purchase finance to encourage consumers to move up the product range. Parts rather than products were standardized – eventually; GM also developed incrementally rather than by grand design.

It is important not to overstress the importance of the Ford strategy as a template which was imposed upon all modern industry. Only the larger-scale mass-production industries such as food, electrical goods, printing and, to some extent, clothing moved towards assembly-line production in the fullest sense. Other industries such as petro-chemicals and steel had certain features in common with the Fordist model by the mid-point of the twentieth century and some, such as pharmaceuticals, followed suit. But some of these industries had highly automated intermediate production stages that make them difficult to assign to a category drawn from an assembly industry such as motor vehicle production.

Nevertheless, three features of the leap forward that Ford's production methods represented are worth highlighting for the illumination they offer to subsequent, more widespread, developments that have occurred most clearly in the period of late modernity. The first of these concerns the effect of Taylorized mass-production methods upon the culture of work. As we have seen, the modern era of industrial production was founded to a large extent on working methods inherited from pre-modern times. Families and communities were important bonding devices enabling the industrial workforces of the large-scale factories, mills and mines to be assembled. Skilled workers were powerful, both upwards with respect to management and the owners of capital, and downwards, with respect to unskilled workers whom they hired. Modernity has been closely associated with the conscious erosion of these sources of economic power, both from management seeking to control industrial expertise and from poorly organized general workers seeking to protect themselves against the arbitrariness of the contracting system. The craft worker, the labour aristocrat, has been squeezed from these two forces almost to extinction.

Secondly, the general worker, unionized into what were to become large-scale labour organizations, particularly in the late-modern period, has had to struggle for incorporation within the modern wage-contract, sometimes against both recalcitrant craft unions and management, sometimes in spite of management blandishments of paternalism or coercion, all of which were, to some extent, deployed in the Ford Motor Corporation. In the process such workers have come to accept that if there is relatively little satisfaction to be had from the labour process itself, deprived as it is of any significant element of control, then it is in the sphere of consumption that psychological satisfactions are to be found. Labour is alienating, yet it produces the means of raising consumption norms. This is despite the efforts of management in many instances to reduce the alienation effect by improving the social relations, relative degree of control and job variety of workers.

Thirdly, industrial capitalism also requires a system of consumption of the kind workers seek as a result of their alienation. If consumption norms are not raised then who can afford to purchase the products of the mass-production system? Gradually, therefore, Fordism spread a recognition of the importance of negotiation and agreement within the corporation, later beyond the corporation into society more generally, in the form of 'collective-bargaining'. This link between production and consumption on a mass scale was also to become a characteristic feature of modernity, one which was one of the more pervasive effects of Fordism.

Fordism beyond the workplace

The linking of mass production to mass consumption is both the great strength and the fatal weakness of modernity. We have seen that its strength is the capacity to generate economic growth through increasing productivity and de-creasing unit costs, thereby in theory expanding the mass market further and further. However, control of the central relationship between production and consumption can no longer remain, as it did at the outset, within the modern corporation since many other corporations, pursuing the same market extension capacity, will influence the operations of the economic system as a whole. In that sense system control moves beyond the grasp of even the largest corporation. Uncertainty regarding the security of the link between production and consumption affects the prepared-ness of firms to invest in new products or production processes; if the rest of society is not enjoying the wage levels of those in the mass-production industries, then once a certain level of demand has been satisfied production may have to be throttled back to prevent overproduction in a context of underconsumption.

The realization that such disequilibria could give rise to severe crisis, potentially capable of destroying the social and economic fabric of modern nation-states, dawned with the slump of the 1930s when productive capacity lay idle and millions of workers were unemployed. Investors would not invest because corporations were making losses, corporations would not invest because they could see no prospect of demand increasing. It was John Maynard Keynes who recognized the lack of an external mechanism capable of righting the relationship. He proposed that responsibility for reviving investor and producer confidence lay with the state because the state had the financial capacity to raise the level of demand in the economy as a whole. By investing in public works projects, for example, the state could create jobs with incomes. Those incomes were the source for increased consumer demand, production would increase once demand had been injected into the ailing economy and consumption deficits would be reduced.

In order to prevent the economy entering recession in the first place Keynes proposed that economies should be regulated by means of controls over levels of taxation, interest rates and budgetary expenditures to 'fine-tune' the economy. This method of regulation became widespread in the advanced economies in the late-modern period and secured levels of economic growth of a kind that had never before been experienced in history. In addition to these government-controlled mechanisms of regulation, certain institutionalized norms regarding the level of income growth in the economy became established.

Interestingly, it was often the unionized workers in the vehicle engineering industry that made the running in establishing these wage norms. This was because substantial parts of the rest of the economy were increasingly feeding inputs into the consumer goods industries, of which cars were an important part. Thus steel workers and rubber, glass and other engineering workers would often take the going rate in the vehicle industry as the norm to which they would aspire in union negotiations with management. The 'wage drift' to which such negotiations gave rise was sustainable during an era of economic, and especially productivity, growth. However it eventually sowed inflationary seeds which were themselves destabilizing when growth slowed down.

Keynesian demand management was coupled to the welfare state in all societies which could be considered advanced during the period of late modernity, Japan being the most obvious exception. There were variations between countries in the precise form taken by the welfare state. In some countries such as Britain and the Scandinavian nations welfare services were extensive, ranging from a centrally supported health service, systems of social security, unemployment insurance, pensions for the retired and publicly funded housing, education and leisure investments. In the USA, the welfare state was less extensive, health provision remained largely private, housing was mainly privately funded, education was largely publicly provided and social services, the vernacular definition of American 'welfare', was focused upon those defined as falling below the poverty line – in other words, the residual poor.

The coupling of demand management and the welfare state was more than simply two parallel forms of state intervention. The Keynesian programme was founded on the idea that, should the economy enter recession or show signs of being likely to do so as measured, for example, by a sharp, short-term rise in unemployment, then public sector investment in construction would be an optimal way of regulating such cyclical effects. Not only would such investment help reduce unemployment directly and rapidly, it would increase demand for building materials such as steel, glass, bricks, cement and so on, thus boosting confidence in those industries and safeguarding or creating employment opportunities in a more indirect way. Moreover, the expansion of the welfare state was itself a major direct contributor to controlling unemployment since most welfare services were labour-intensive. Clearly, therefore, the welfare state could be seen as a major set of institutions having both a substantial effect upon improving quality of life for the broad range of citizens, and helping to keep unemployment at historically low levels. During the 1950s and 1960s unemployment in Britain, for example, seldom rose much above 3 per cent in even the least wealthy regions, and on average it was at or around 1–2 per cent. Effectively the Keynesian welfare mode of socio-economic regulation meant that there was no unemployment.

It has been argued by some radical analysts from the political Left that the welfare state was primarily a device aimed at subsidizing modern capitalism. Corporations benefited from having a healthier, better educated workforce, and they clearly benefited from the welfare-state effects of the economic regulator which raised demand at uncertain times in the business cycle, as this was a direct source of profit for those companies supplying the needs of the welfare state. Modern capitalism could not function without the instruments of the state mode of regulation in its managerial or welfare forms. However, such arguments, while having some obvious truth to them, overestimated the centrality of the welfare state to modern capitalism and underestimated the political pressure from those in need of better housing, health and welfare services which caused the state in many countries to expand provision.

It seems likely that the welfare institutions of the modern nation state were, and thus far remain, a classic compromise arising from the logic of modernity expressed through the conflictual party system of a democratic society. If modernity did imply equality of rights and liberties for the individual within the framework of an authoritative, legitimate sovereign state, then eventually, once the citizen's rights to representation in the workplace and electoral system had been accepted, the right to equality in welfare and other collective entitlements would be the next step for an enfranchised electorate. Where such electorates were strongly infused with social democratic ideologies, as in north-west Europe, welfare states became strongly pronounced. Where they were not, as in the USA and in Japan, they were less pronounced or largely absent. The modern welfare state was the product of unevenly developed political pursuit of welfare rights. If it had been opposed to the interests of capital in an objective sense it is doubtful whether it would have developed as far as it did. That capital under conditions of modernity does not require a full-blooded welfare state to survive is testified by the historic experience of the USA and Japan, and to some extent by the recent history of welfarism in Britain and some other European countries where the growth rate in key services has been reined in.

An important element of the welfare programme in modern north-west European nation-states has been the provision of public or social housing. Moreover, in some of those countries, Britain being a clear case in point, there has also been public subsidy through tax relief on mortgage interest to the private housing sector. The house-building programme was a major element in the state mode of regulation under what the French 'Regulation School' of economic theorists have called the Fordist 'regime of accumulation'. A state interventionist mode of regulation, buttressed by the institution of collective bargaining and extending during some periods when capital, organized labour and the state secured a 'social contract' through 'corporatist' agreement, can be seen as fitting together with a Fordist, mass-consumption 'regime of accumulation' (or form of profit maximization) in three specific ways with regard to housing policy.

In the first instance, the renewal of the urban environment and construction of new, large-scale suburbs creates secondary demand for the consumer durables so typical of modernistic lifestyles. Whereas older forms of housing may have at best a neutral effect upon consumer demand because of the inappropriateness of design in relation to the space demands of modern appliances, new housing normally requires the installation of advanced domestic appliances. As Le Corbusier, the leading architect of modernism, noted, 'the house is a machine for living in'. Such 'machines' require mechanized consumption goods to function at maximum efficiency. State housing expansion in the period from the late 1950s to the mid-1970s stimulated a huge growth in demand for washing machines, refrigerators, cars and electronic audio-visual equipment, thereby boosting the level of domestic production as well as imports.

Secondly, the construction of mass housing, especially high-density high- or low-rise dwellings, stimulated the construction industry to seek greater efficiency and productivity. The demand for rapid construction of very large blocks of flats outstripped the capacity of traditional building methods to cope. The construction industry had, therefore, to increase its level of capital intensity by investment in large-scale construction equipment, cranes and, not least, new building technologies. Thus construction firms created secondary demand in the engineering industry for innovative products, such as earth-moving machines, which were also capable of successful marketing overseas. Such machinery was also capable of being linked with Fordist raw material production methods such as mobile, ready-mixed cement and system-building panels, prefabricated in factory conditions. With hindsight it is clear that in Britain, at least, the pace of technological development under Fordism in the construction industry was too rapid to allow the development of training and skills in the workforce to keep pace. As a consequence some elements of the impact of modernization in the construction industry now appear to have been counter-productive. However, other elements – notably the increase in capital intensiveness and the related organization of building labour into a more industrialized workforce capable of collective bargaining over wages and conditions – contributed to the relative success of the British construction industry domestically and overseas during the Fordist period.

The third connection between the Keynesian welfare mode of regulation and the Fordist regime of accumulation is that subsidized housing provided a social wage to the workforce. This subvention, composed not only of housing subsidy through rent reduction or tax relief on mortgage interest but also of other welfare disbursements such as child benefit, offset the level of wage demand in the economy. That is not to say that collective bargaining under Fordism did not focus substantially upon wages issues. However, the level at which trades unions would settle wages disputes with employers was influenced by the existence of the social wage. Sometimes this was overtly the case, as during the period of the 'social contract' in Britain in the 1970s, and more formally in Scandinavian 'corporatist' forms of negotiation. More often it was simply assumed as a normal element in overall wage negotiations. As a consequence costs of a direct kind to employers were kept fractionally less than they would otherwise have been, thus assisting their efforts to remain competitive overseas.

The geographical structures of Fordism

The factories of Fordist production were often situated in new industrial spaces. The early Ford plants at Piquette Point and Highland Park were in Detroit. But space requirements meant that the giant River Rouge plant had to be located outside the city but close enough to the labour pools it offered. In time, suburbia grew out to meet the plants, by which time management had centralized the headquarter offices in the separate locality of Dearborn, Michigan. Modernity is a restless condition and Fordism is a hyperactive regime of capital accumulation. In Britain, Ford was one of the early inward investors, arriving to cross the tariff barriers of imperial preference in the 1920s. Locating briefly at Trafford Park, the new industrial space on the fringes of Manchester, the company quickly moved to a new, vertically integrated production complex at Dagenham, just outside the major market and labour pool of London. One of the larger, interwar mass housing schemes funded by the public sector was constructed at Dagenham to house Fordist workers. Later, truck construction began at Langley, Buckinghamshire, in 1961, then in 1963 a whole new complex was opened at Halewood, near Liverpool. Just as with Dearborn, Michigan, the headquarters of Ford (Britain) moved to Warley, Essex, in 1964 and a year later tractor production moved to Basildon, Essex. An axle and power-train plant was opened in Swansea in Wales in 1965 followed in 1978 by an engine plant at Bridgend. Welsh operations were expanded by a new £600 million investment in lean-burn engine technology announced in 1988.

Over a 30-year period, the Ford Motor Company had consolidated in its Home Counties core (though some of its vertically integrated functions closed there in the 1980s) and established major outposts first along the major geographical axis of growth in Britain in the 1960s, the London–Merseyside belt, then down its new axis of growth in the 1980s, the M4

73

Figure 4 Southern consolidation.

corridor into Wales. Decision-making on investment is as restless as the needle on a radar screen and encompasses a European, North American and increasingly global perspective over time.

The spatial activities of corporate entities cannot be reduced to, only illuminated by, the practices of one of the major players. But it is instructive that other British-based vehicle producers also began exploring distant territory in the 1960s. What is now the Rover Group opened new plants in Wales, Merseyside and Scotland in the 1960s, and what is now Peugeot also located new investment in Scotland at the same time. All were closed during the 1980s. Only General Motors' new plant on Merseyside remains in place from this clutch of modernization and expansion plans. Ford has been less capricious in its spatial strategy, though its preference for the M4 over the M1 development axis seems to be consolidating.

Other industries centred in early modern cities were also to be seen shifting their locations either out of those cities completely or to complementary locations in under-industrialized areas or those which had been major centres of capital accumulation and trade in the early modern period. Electrical and electronics firms such as Ferranti opened branches in Scotland and Wales, as did Thorn Electrical in Wales and north-east England. A textiles giant such as Courtaulds pursued a similar strategy, rationalizing employment in established textile regions and opening new branches in Wales, Northern Ireland and the north-east. Foreign investors such as IBM, Honeywell and Burroughs followed suit as did DuPont and Monsanto in their investment and location strategies. Some, if not all, of these 1960s investments had also been reversed by the 1980s.

How did this happen, and what was being sought? It is impossible to understand this reformation of the space economy, the industrial geography of late modern Britain, without an understanding of the state mode of regulation of the capitalist development process. As David Harvey has

75

pointed out, capital has an ineluctable dynamic to move over space, penetrating new accumulation resources and opportunities, relinquishing sites of earlier accumulation success in a process of ever-increasing, restless effort to release itself from the geographical structures – cities and regions – to which it once gave birth but now finds constraining. Labour, usually put in place by this process, especially in the labour-intensive era of early modernity, has an interest in maintaining its *in situ* strength. There is little except individual career enhancement to be achieved by geographical mobility for the Fordist worker. Investment has been made in social and communal networks, cultural capital and housing. Moreover, labour's only strength to resist capital is its solidarity which is cemented by labour organizations established in spatially distinctive areas. As we have seen, such resistance is at loggerheads with the locust-like mobility of capitalist modernity. If the contradiction between stability and mobility is to be resolved the powers of the third party of the sovereign state have often to be invoked to regulate the development of tendencies towards crisis.

The late modern state has regulated such regional crises in three main ways. First of all, and under conditions of substantial consensus between the major contending political parties, the state regulated the freedom of capital to move over space. At various times approval to expand in the urban fringe of the London area has been refused but subsidy has been offered to the same firms if they agree to move to areas of high unemployment in the deindustrializing centres of early modernity – northern England, Scotland, South Wales. When the Ford Motor Company moved to Wales in the 1970s the state paid virtually the total cost of equipping the new complex, and on average a sum of £30 000–£40 000 has been paid for every job created in the areas receiving inward investment assistance. But firms do not simply respond to such state injunctions, they have to be assured that such moves are going to be economically efficient by saving on labour costs and increasing productivity.

On some occasions, though not for long periods, state regulation has involved subsidizing wage costs in a direct way by paying a premium for every *male* worker taken into employment by a firm moving into an assisted area. But, more generally, such subsidies have come through the operation of the social wage, particularly in the provision of housing by the public sector. House-building policies have at various times been especially concentrated in areas of high unemployment, not simply through the construction of new housing estates but of complete new towns and the large-scale expansion of existing towns. During the era of late modernity such housing was available for rent at less than the market rate, a factor which assisted the maintenance of relatively depressed wage costs in such areas. Such policies have also applied in the more developed cities but other factors, such as localized union solidarity and local inflation in living standards, have in the past offset the wage-cost advantage in the more developed urban settings.

The third regulatory intervention has been the construction of a modern infrastructure, especially roads, linking the more distant parts of the national territory to the command centres in or near the capital and thereafter to the wider domestic and overseas markets. It is doubtful whether so much regional investment would have taken place under the Fordist accumulation regime had spatial distance not been reduced substantially by temporal improvements in state subsidized road and, it should not be forgotten, rail transport. Because the modern state had to hold the ring between the conflicting interests of capital and labour, it met at various times and in changing ways at least the minimum requirements of both. It thereby minimized the social crisis tendencies implicit in the dislocations of spatial development under the restless conditions of modernity.

But these geographical compromises and structural changes are limited to the scale of the nation-state. Fordism has long transcended the reach of the single nation-state; it now operates on a global level. As the advantages offered by the less developed regions of the modern nation-states became increasingly marginal, and the productive capacity of Fordist enterprise outstripped the markets of the advanced world, so location on a global scale was more fully explored. Again, the leading industries constructing the new global networks tended to be in motor vehicle production, electrical and electronic engineering and the textile industry. Multinational production organization gave rise to a phenomenon termed the 'new international division of labour'. It supplemented the older international system whereby former colonial territories supplied staple goods and raw materials to the advanced countries where they were processed into finished articles for consumption principally in the markets of the developed world.

The new international division of labour involved the extension of Fordist networks through the export of capital invested in the implantation of branch factories in the very low wage economies of the less developed countries. In the Americas, such countries as Mexico, Brazil and Argentina were recipients of both North American and European branch factories involved principally in the assembly of ready-made components into finished consumer goods. In Europe, the southern countries of Spain and Portugal, and the Italian *Mezzogiorno*, were similarly recipients of European and North American consumer industry investments. Later North African countries were joined into the branch plant economy of Fordism as German and French textile and engineering companies discovered their value as export platforms.

Elsewhere, South-East Asian countries such as Singapore, South Korea, Hong Kong and Taiwan have become incorporated into the textile and electronics industrial networks of Japanese, North American and European companies seeking locations where labour-intensive assembly operations can be carried out cheaply. As such locations have been subject to wage cost rises, locations in cheaper labour markets such as

Thailand, the Philippines and Indonesia have been sought. In some cases, localized development has occurred, again in concert with local, state modes of regulation to limit labour organization and subsidize investment, so that some less developed countries have become 'newly industrializing countries' capable of acting as markets as well as producers of Fordist consumer goods. Moreover, local competitors and sub-contractors have emerged as income levels and expertise from Fordist industry have filtered into the wider society.

Hence, by the 1970s Fordism had become entrenched as a global regime of accumulation. The decomposition of the labour process explicit in its early industrial organizational style had enabled control and command to be retained centrally while the distinctive parts of the production process were decentralized internationally. In the process, the consumption norms of western modernity were increasingly generalized as new locations became consumers as well as producers of Fordist industry. In every case the global regime of accumulation relied on the carefully constructed complementarities of localized modes of state regulation. Increasingly, those states able to regulate the practices of labour most strenuously became the favoured recipients of new investment. As in Henry Ford's original factory, the struggle to maintain the compliance of the labour force was of paramount importance to the project of modernity.

The crisis of global Fordism

The movement in the 1970s of Fordist industry towards the less developed world signalled the beginning of a severe crisis in the regime of accumulation. According to Alain Lipietz, a member of the French regulation school of economic theorists, the move was caused by a slowdown in profitability caused by a decrease in the rate of productivity gains in typical Fordist industries such as the production of motor vehicles. Decreasing productivity first provoked increased investment in advanced capital goods. There followed attempts to increase worker productivity by increasing worker participation and, to limited degrees, worker involvement and control in the production process. These technological and social changes were termed 'neo-Fordist' since they represented a more developed form of the initial Fordist ideas of task differentiation and supervision. However these changes did not result in sufficient productivity increases to offset the scale of investment in production. Moreover, wage costs were also rising as part of the collective bargaining agreements involved in the new production methods. In partial consequence of these changes, unemployment began rising and western economies began to be characterized by the combination of stagnation and inflation, the latter provoked in part by growing indebtedess in the private and public sectors.

But the source of the productivity crisis lay within the Fordist production process itself. The removal of expertise from the shopfloor worker and the centralization of strategic information within an increasingly bureaucratized hierachy of control meant that problems arising at shopfloor level took an increasingly long time to resolve. This was exacerbated by the increasingly sophisticated technology used in the manufacturing process. Thus the amount of time that the assembly line was stationary, the time taken to retool machinery, and the consequent delays in producing finished vehicles contributed in important ways to the productivity problem. The limits of Fordist technology and labour organization were being reached. These problems were particularly pronounced in the home of Fordism, the USA, and added to by the efficiency of new competitors, notably West Germany and Japan, whose levels of productivity began to outstrip American unit labour costs. Comparable problems beset the British consumer goods sectors, and trade balances began to show deficits. The oil crisis of 1973 reinforced these tendencies.

Competition became heightened as the domestic markets

of the weaker economies were assailed by the products of the stronger ones. Japan, in particular, began building on its domestic market strength by pursuing a series of export drives. In the European countries a common response to inflation and recession was to pursue policies to curb what was perceived as the source of inflation, rising wage costs, thus limiting the purchasing power of domestic consumers at the same time as seeking to further develop overseas markets. Because of quality problems and a failure sufficiently to invest domestically and overseas in countries where low wage costs might temporarily allay productivity problems, Britain suffered most in this period. France and West Germany, both pursuing a more global investment strategy in Fordist industries, were less negatively affected. As previously noted, some newly industrializing countries, borrowing from the west to support inward investment in Fordist industry, then re-exporting output to the west, showed spectacular rates of economic growth.

But none of them was able fully to make the vital link in the chain between Fordist labour processes and western wage levels and consumption norms. Hence the general re-exporting strategy tended further to feed markets which were already reaching saturation point. In some of these newly industrializing countries, especially those dependent on raw materials as collateral for western indebtedness, the Fordist strategy failed when the price of oil was substantially raised yet again in 1979, reducing demand and with it oil revenues. The simultaneous introduction of monetarist policies of high interest rates to squeeze inflation out of the system in the USA and key European economies forced many such countries into a level of debt that was self-defeating for them and their creditors. Only the non-oil-producing, newly industrializing countries, mostly in South-East Asia, escaped this fate.

In those economies that had practised counter-recessionary Keynesian demand management policies, the inflationary implications of that mode of regulation meant that it was

81

being rejected extremely rapidly; and at the corporate level, the institution of collective bargaining was increasingly coming under attack. The relative power of labour organizations to enforce the Fordist link between production and consumption was also being undermined as national governments, particularly in the British case, introduced legislation curbing union rights. US firms began exploring the southern strategy, moving geographically to areas of the country where labour traditions were less antagonistic or where local 'right-to-work' legislation prevailed.

Western producers began to look eastwards at the practices of the supremely successful Japanese form of mass production. This had proved capable of exporting better quality, more reliable and cheaper consumer goods to the heartland of Fordist production. The Ford Motor Company revised its 'world car' strategy of the 1970s by adopting an 'AJ strategy' standing for 'After Japan'. This entailed looking closely at the prospects for further reducing unit labour costs by reducing employment levels and requiring remaining workers to work harder on a wider range of work tasks. The domestically owned British car industry experienced extreme difficulties during the recessionary period of the early 1980s. Fordist industry everywhere in Britain was subjected to a massive shakeout, involving plant closures, deindustrialization of established manufacturing centres, and weakening of trades union involvement. Industries that had been strongly dependent on Keynesian state shareholding or ownership were subjected to the harsher disciplines of the open market as neoconservative ideology contributed to more general problems with a 'survival of the fittest' ideology. It seemed as though the whole interlocking support system of economic modernity was under threat as a way out of the crisis was sought through the application of monetarist principles.

Such principles were also to be extended to the social wage goods hitherto enjoyed by Fordist workers. Economic rents began to be charged for public sector housing. A strategy of reducing public sector responsibility in the housing sphere was pursued by the twin policies of privatization of ownership to individual occupiers and limitation of the autonomy of municipalities to construct new public sector housing. Other welfare state responsibilities of local councils such as social services and education expenditure were to be severely curtailed, and the centralized welfare state itself came under ideological attack. However, the increasing levels of unemployment and poverty occasioned by the monetarist shakeout meant that welfare expenditure, particularly on unemployment benefit, rose to historically high levels, indicating the extreme difficulty of uncoupling the public–private mutuality that had typified the era of the mixed economy.

In its stead, once inflation had been tamed, has been inserted a neo-Keynesian policy of cheapening credit to encourage a consumer boom, increasingly satisfied by imports from the economically more successful producers of mass-consumption goods. Employment in the burgeoning service sector, notably in financial and other private services, continued to grow while that in manufacturing declined substantially during the recession years of the 1980s.

The Fordist worker of yesteryear may now find herself or himself early retired, unemployed or more casually employed on a part-time or occasional full-time basis. The individualistic spirit of modernity is widely celebrated in efforts to regenerate a Victorian idealization of the 'enterprise culture' expressed in support for small businesses and the freedom from bureaucratic control implied by the Fordist-Keynesian compact of old. The consumer with sufficient income is encouraged to express her or his individuality by rejecting the standardized products of Fordist industry and purchasing more customized, 'designer' items; the mass markets of Fordist output have increasingly been broken down into market segments constructed around the ability to pay.

Such changes have forced a reconsideration of the

appropriateness of Fordism as a regime of accumulation at the highest levels of corporate and political life as markets are perceived increasingly as the driving force of economies in which producer sovereignty has begun to give way to a more strongly defined consumer sovereignty. The implications of such discoveries remain unclear for the present, but that they are of considerable significance for the idea of progress contained within the project of modernity seems indisputable. Some observers have expressed the thought that progress as understood most clearly in the link between the Keynesian welfare state and the Fordist regime of accumulation with its premium on the minimization of unemployment contained, with inflation, the seeds of its own destruction. How is social progress to be understood in a context of growing social and income polarisation? Has the project of modernity come to an exhausted end, or is it merely held on pause? Questions such as these will be explored in the second half of this book.

CHAPTER FOUR

The question of postmodernity

Modernism under fire

In the Prins Hendriklaan in Utrecht, at the eastern end of a rather bleak row of nineteenth-century villas built in brown brick, is a house of startling appearance. It is a low, two-storey, brilliantly white, stuccoed, flat-roofed construction, its austere planes divided by colour lines painted in primary yellow, red and blue. The house is reminiscent of a painting by Mondrian and, indeed, it turns out to belong to the Dutch cultural movement called De Stijl, of which Mondrian was a founder member. The house (featured on the cover) is the Rietveld Schröder House, designed by Gerrit Rietveld for Truus Schröder and her three children. It was built in 1924, and consists of a small kitchen, hall and study on the ground floor, the kitchen quite traditionally designed, and a single, large living room on the second floor, divisible into three bedrooms by a system of sliding walls; the bathroom also expands by means of a sliding wall. The austere external colour scheme is repeated but interpreted more boldly inside, with a red-painted floor and a black ceiling. The windows of the house are horizontal, rejecting the vertical line of traditional design, and some of the windows continue round the corner of the building, leaving the roof seemingly floating. The furniture is Rietveld's design, the zigzag chair being the centrepiece. The whole ensemble is symbolic of the rebellious resistance to the past that

85

aesthetic modernism represented. The Rietveld Schröder house is now a museum.

Is the fact that an icon of modernity should end up being treated *as* an icon, visited, analysed, exhaustively written about in numerous books, of significance? After all, it is normal to expect to see Mondrian's paintings in any museum of modern art, along with those representative of the other great modernist movements, cubism, expressionism, surrealism, futurism and so on. At least it has not been demolished or blown up as some other less celebrated products of architectural modernism have in recent years. In 1987, its first full year as a museum, it attracted 10 000 visitors. The house is not as it was when last lived in, in 1985. The modifications that were made during sixty years of domestic use, an upstairs kitchen, variations in decoration, installation of new domestic appliances and furnishings, have been removed. There is no TV set, a 1920s gramophone has been reinstalled in Rietveld's chinese box of a home entertainment unit, there are no cushions on the Rietveld chair. The house is now another exercise in hyper-reality. It is more 'real', more austere, more authentic to the ideals of modernity than it was for the largest part of its residential existence. It has been distanced, restored, its purpose changed selectively to capture modernity as part of a wider story, a grander narrative of progress through stark opposition to tradition.

Perhaps this is the meaning of the Rietveld Schröder House museum, the representation of a moment of modernity, the return of aura to an original aesthetic form, the logic of which has been exhausted by its de-formed reproduction in innumerable twentieth-century houses, blocks of flats, offices and factories. We may be tired of the copies but fascinated by their origins. Such thinking seems recently to have permeated popular opinion. A great debate has opened up with the intervention of the Prince of Wales into the hitherto closed professional controversy over architectural form. He has touched a chord of popular disaffection with his dismissal of the functionalist austerity of modernist buildings. Eighty per cent of those polled after a television broadcast, in which modernist designs were vilified as anything from incinerators to word processors, not to mention monstrous carbuncles, agreed with his judgement.

But what are his prescriptions? There seem to be two. Architecture should not reject but revere the past, above all the pre-modern past. Thus a classical design such as St Paul's cathedral should not be hemmed in with the spare and functional lines of modernism, it should be made the centrepiece of a piazza fringed with well-mannered, neo-classical, pillared and pedimented building designs. London's skyline should be returned to its Renaissance profile of low-rise buildings punctuated only by church spires giving due architectural deference to the magnificence of St Paul's. Quinlan Terry's neoclassical parade of shops and offices recently completed at Richmond, south London, would be the exemplar.

Secondly, people should be able to control the design of their own housing. Instead of being forced to live in modernist towers and flats in the ubiquitous public housing estates of the 1960s, the ordinary householder should be able to engage in 'community architecture'. Thus, in place of the fear and alienation imposed upon the flat-dweller by deck-access routeways, darkened tunnels, and malfunctioning lifts there should be small-scale refurbishment of older houses mixed in with sensitively designed new infill developments which protect and nurture a communal sense of pride and sociability. Architects should not impose their egos upon their clients but be socially and aesthetically responsive to public needs and aspirations. They should not only work but live amongst the people whose houses they have helped to design.

The appeal to ideas of community and the authority of tradition is clearly a populist yet also a reactionary one. It is not simply a postmodernist position, it is an example of what Frederic Jameson, an American critic, has called reactionary anti-modernism. In the light of the earlier discussion on the incompatibility between community and modernity, the connection between community architecture and anti-modernism is at least a consistent, if romantic one. The question of power structures, interests and influences in contemporary society is, however, not addressed in the critique except implicitly. Is modernity and the democratic impulse that has been a central part of it to be replaced by some authoritarian, neo-absolutist impulse? There is in reactionary anti-modernism, also in the politics of neo-conservatism, a yearning for the return to the values of discipline, acceptance of authority and a rejection of social engineering. Yet neoconservatism is riven by the contradict-ory ideology of individual freedom to choose amongst the alternatives presented by the market, subject only to the ability to pay. Such freedoms can include the desire to construct a modernist monument in the heart of the financial district in the City of London or the postmodernist 'wireless set' that could be its substitute. The debate is thus a complex one and it certainly transcends mere architecture. The survival, perhaps the resurgence, of modernity in the face of what appears to be its present impasse demands the unteasing of these complexities, a critical appraisal of its discontents, and a delineation of its prospects in what presently can appear to be a hostile climate.

Postmodern thinking and the problem of philosophy

A number of books have been published in the late 1980s with titles which suggest that the work of philosophers is over, their subject has come to an end, there is no point in continuing because the problem they thought they were grappling with was in fact not a problem at all but a mystification. Some philosophers have given up their university posts, most have not, though others have found the status of their departments downgraded. Meanwhile the status of departments of English, especially those containing expertise in advanced literary criticism, has increased. This change is not merely coincidental. Since the late 1960s a war of words between philosophers and literary critics has led to victory going, for the moment, to the latter. What was this war about and why should some philosophers have been amongst the loudest advocates of their own possible demise? The war was fought, as many others have been, over who or what was to decide the truth; but unlike most wars, in which truth has been the first casualty, this one may have seen truth as the last casualty.

In our commonsense way, we take the truth of a statement to be the degree to which it equates with our experience. Or, if the statement seems to conflict with our experience, and if sufficient experts tell us of the invalidity of our perception, we might, in time, change our experience – surprising as that may seem. Common-sense of this kind is, however, a modern way of thinking. It was not always so and it still is not so in many parts of the world. In the middle ages, for example, when cosmology was part of religion, the biblical focus on the divine creation meant that no one questioned the centrality of the earth in the universe. It seemed obvious that the sun revolved around the earth. This belief complied with the impression gained by watching the movement of the sun across the sky. The observer, or subject, could apply a law-like statement – the sun revolves around the earth – to the natural process, the object, taking place outside, and check its validity, its truthfulness. There could be little difficulty in agreeing to the truthfulness of the statement because nature could be seen complying with it. The statement was true; subject and object, though separate, had been reconciled.

Except, of course, that they hadn't. The law was wrong, the subject was mistaken, the object was doing the opposite to what it seemed. Knowledge was based not on truth but its opposite. When Copernicus discovered that the earth was not the centre of the cosmos it was a dangerous heresy that struck at the heart of theological knowledge. The development of thinking during the Enlightenment in the seventeenth and eighteenth centuries hinged upon the debate about the truth of Copernican theory. This debate was carried out most forcefully between Galileo and his detractors. The method of determining the truth scientifically, which was discovered by Copernicus (and elaborated by others), became in turn a definition of reason. Philosophy subsequently became the guardian of this method of discovering the truth. Reason became the means of enabling such truth to be corroborated. Measurement became the technique for demonstrating the invincibility of the truth.

Philosophers, from Descartes onwards, sought to show that the methods of reason were the superior form of establishing objective truth. They were, of course, not the only methods and not methods to which moral or aesthetic judgements could be subjected, but such judgements might aspire to the rational quality of scientific method. Yet this 'mirror of nature' method of reconciling subjective to objective truth, as Richard Rorty terms it, has come under attack. A number of writers and philosophers are dissatisfied with it. The mirror imagery tells us that the mind of the subject is a mirror held up to the objective world. In the mirror are representations of the world, and where the image is clouded the subject must look inwards to improve reception by adjusting the rule-governed relationship between image and reality.

Yet it is the rules of rational method that pose the key problem. Where do they come from? How applicable are they in contexts different from the European and western centres of philosophy where they are safeguarded? Let us take an example, a common one used to demonstrate the power of western rationalism. Consider the statement: 'all swans are white'. On first appearance this may seem true until one remembers the black swan seen in the zoo. In which case the revised truth about swans is contained in the statement: 'not all swans are white'. This is how western knowledge proceeds, by proposition, testing, corroboration, refutation until some truthful, law-like statement is arrived at. It is also a pictorial way of reasoning: we can picture a swan, we know it is not a sparrow, we can decode the text of the statement. But if one were to take the statements, let us say, to Australia and ask an Aboriginal to confirm or deny either of them on the basis of his or her experience, then the question might be meaningless. Birds are not classified in a comparable way to that of the west, a different code is in operation, the question does not arise. Neither statement constitutes knowledge.

Now, a common response to that situation is to say that Aboriginal culture is less developed than our own, that were it to become as developed as western culture, then such distinctions and classifications would eventually develop. Thus for the moment we assume our western knowledge to be superior, more sophisticated, than that of others who do not share our codes for picturing reality. It is such Eurocentric thinking that is central to the philosophical critique of modernity. That may seem madness. Why jettison the cornucopia of knowledge and its products that western reasoning has brought to the world. Why indeed? But how is that knowledge justified, except in terms of itself, who makes the rules, and are they indeed rules?

It is at this point that another and more serious attack on the foundations of western scientific reason is encountered. The American philosopher Thomas Kuhn proposed, most controversially in the 1960s, that scientists often do not follow the supposed rules that philosophers sought to safeguard as the embodiment of reason. Scientific discoveries were sometimes made by accident, by a wild guess or even mystical belief. When such discoveries had been tested and found to be valid the scientist often had difficulty in convincing his peers of their validity, particularly where the new knowledge challenged the prevailing professional consensus. Editorial boards might then prevent the publication of findings, and without publication the scientist might find it hard to gain employment. In other words, scientific activity was often characterized by a conspiracy to maintain the consensus regarding 'normally' accepted truth because to do otherwise might rock the boat. This, of course, is reminiscent of the reception given by theologians to Copernican theory. Scientific knowledge, too, is a belief system based on specific conversations or texts. To overturn such texts requires the development amongst an 'out-group' of a counter-discourse.

This suggested that truth, if it lay anywhere, lay in language. But are the words that make up language themselves representative of reality or do they take their meaning from other words? Here, perhaps, is the knife edge in the critique and defence of modern thought. Many twentieth-century philosophers have accepted the idea that language analysis is the best means of deciding what is true knowledge and what is not. One strand of thinking was to treat knowledge as logic, whereby only logical statements could be ascribed meaning, and illogical ones would be literally meaningless. The fact that a sentence such as 'colours have different weights' is both logical and meaning-less suggests why that approach was sidetracked. A reaction against this was to develop the idea that the task of philosophy was to determine the truth of sentences by their relations with one another, to establish the ways in which the actual practice of speaking true sentences was carried out. A different reaction has been to say that language refers to entities or events in reality, that it pictures some part of the world in which we are interested. However, Wittgenstein had anticipated the problem with that approach in his notion of language as a 'game', where meaning derives from the use we make of words and sentences rather than some capacity thought has of picturing meaning directly from reality.

The question thus becomes one of how such language games come into being. The answer is that they arise, parasitically perhaps, in opposition to the systematic bodies of thought which seek to provide a universal statement about the true way of discovering knowledge. Just as Copernicus and Galileo confronted the accepted truths which preceded them, thereby creating a new language game, so those who oppose the idea that it is possible for language to represent reality create a new code within which to discuss that truth. It can easily be argued that such subversion of the rules ought not to gather many adherents in support of it if it fails to show, as Copernicus did, the ways in which the old rules no longer fit reality. But those philosophers who argue that words function in relation to each other rather than representing the objective world are, unlike Copernicus or Galileo, rejecting the idea of philosophy as a method for representing the world. They wish to argue there are no philosophical foundations for getting at the truth about reality. They do not deny the existence of reality, merely that language connects internally to itself rather than to the world.

The criticism of this view is that it is relativistic. How are we to know that those who adhere to a particular language game, trapped inside their language bubble, understand reality better than those outside it? This is the essence of the debate between Jürgen Habermas and post-structuralist writers such as Foucault and Derrida. Habermas agrees that language is crucial because its character as a medium of communication enables the truth of statements to be adjudicated by means of argument. Importantly, though, he insists upon agreement about what are to be the rules of reasoned debate. Without acceptance of the foundations of what is to be allowed the status of 'knowledge', the achievement of consensus is impossible. If communication occurs in such a way that what it refers to can never be established with certainty then language has lost its meaning.

The French writers Derrida, Foucault and Lyotard refused Habermas' central assumption that truth has philosophical foundations. For Foucault, truth is established by the exercise of power; knowledge is always contested and the desire for knowledge is equally a desire for power. In particular, he criticized the way that the individual subject has been made so central to the development of western forms of knowledge. First, it separated distinctive kinds of ~~subjective judgements of superiority and inferiority. Third,~~ 'normal' society. Second, scientific classification produced subjective judgements of superiority and inferiority. Thirdly, this encouraged subjective definitions of identity based on everyday perceptions of superiority and inferiority. These local discourses of power became totalizing in their definition of 'normality'. Moreover, the fact that such perceptions could change, not solely by virtue of scientific reason, but by the exercise of power, as in the cases of class, racial or gender inequality, made Habermas' notion of a transparent, value-free concept of reason an untenable one. Foucault saw his task as interrogating the localized ways in which that concept of reason developed and was applied.

Derrida has invented the idea of 'deconstruction' as the equivalent technique for interrogating what, for him, are the only real residues of the quest for knowledge, the texts that authors produce. Deconstruction is like reversing a tapestry to show the threads behind in all their complexity and apparent incomprehensibility, revealing the diverse sources by which a particular representation of reality is composed. The threads, for Derrida, are 'traces' from other texts which reveal knowledge as nothing more or less than a product of 'intertextuality'. Lyotard, who has criticized both the totalizing nature of modern rationality with its 'grand narratives', and its spurious foundationalism, has advocated a provisional philosophy of 'local narratives' ungoverned by general rules, critical of the grand institutions and structures of thought which are expressive of modern society, but also conscious of the limits of language within a basically intertextual domain.

Thus, with the intervention of Lyotard, we reach the beginnings of a definition of postmodernity. Postmodern thinking is critical of the general, centralized, purposive and distanced characteristics of modern thought. The author,

Figure 5 The new battle of the books.

while being responsible for the texts produced, is relegated to a secondary position, decentred, in favour of the relationships between texts. Knowledge derives from the interrogation of texts, seeking their hidden modes of domination, looking, for example, for their local exclusions on questions of gender, ethnicity, geography and so on. If postmodern thinking has a purpose it is an ironic, subversive one, not necessarily a positive or reforming one. And in place of the distance between dominant thinking and the hegemony of rules it envisions a more participatory, conversational mode of reasoning.

It is fairly easy to see that, despite claims to the contrary, the mode of thinking which is increasingly called postmodern does not break in any significant way with that which it claims to have superseded. The focus on language is accepted by modernists and postmodernists alike, the difference is that the latter mainly wish to interrogate the assumptions embedded in the discourse of modernity. Without that discourse, or discourses, postmodern thought has nothing upon which to attach itself or to deconstruct. The exploration of the margins, the attempt to bring under inspection the knowledges that are subsumed under the grand narratives of modernity, is unquestionably an advance but these are modes of thinking which seem unlikely to overthrow such narratives even though they may challenge them to be more democratic. It seems unlikely, therefore, that postmodern modes of thinking can have a similar problematic effect upon the modern concept of reason to that posed for the theological mode of understanding reality by the Copernican revolution. The stakes are too high, the dangers posed by jettisoning the foundations of modern thought, arbitrary though they may be, too great. For if the relativism implicit in purely local reasoning becomes the standard, then the exercise of power becomes the arbiter of truth. Postmodern thought is predicated precisely upon the critique of such outcomes, thus it is complicit with the project of modernity.

Postmodern fiction

If the claims that language philosophy in the contemporary period has made a complete break with modern philosophy seem ambitious, those that postmodern writing has done the same, or gone even further from its modern progenitor, are even more so. As we shall see, however, the degree of crossover between philosophy and literary criticism is now quite remarkable, with the latter's exponents habitually using the language of the former to account for what is going on and vice versa. It is this element of crossover that is one of the more interesting innovations in contemporary thinking, and one which is not limited solely to the disciplinary relations between philosophy and literary criticism. It can be found, to varying degrees, in relations between geography and sociology; sociology, cultural studies and psychology; and economics, philosophy and literary criticism. Central to all these crossovers is the fundamental idea that the way thought is written exerts a pervasive effect on the truth value of what is being communicated. The roles of rhetoric and what is often called the 'poetics' of writing are now recognized as both problematic and interesting scientific questions. Poetics refers to the imagery and patterns of thought that organize the way discourse about the world is presented in the text.

For example, in what has been noted already about certain characteristics of modernist thinking and writing we can see a number of elements that contribute to its poetics. The subject is seen as the conscious, creative interpreter of reality, governed in these interpretations by rules derived from the central authority of a respected school of thought. The culture within which that subject is embedded can be seen as somewhat monolithic with respect to its image of the 'normal' subject: a white, male, propertied citizen. Those deriving identity from other characteristics, black, female or non-western might expect to be marginalized. Art had, first, the duty of edifying the elite social groups of modern society, then, primarily, a duty to itself – 'art for art's sake' – rather than an inclusive, communicative function. The poetics of history expressed a narrative of continuity, evolution or revolution by stages to some purposive end. In philosophy, there was for most of the modern era a dominant belief in the capacity of subjective thought to deal, albeit problematically, with the world 'out there'. There were foundations to ways of getting at the truth.

Postmodern poetics, it is argued by some, have overturned all that. Foucault's questions about the subject have led to a decentred view of the role of the subject. An example is the way the narrator in contemporary fiction often seems to step outside the narrative and address the reader, or may, indeed, take on a multiplicity of different perspectives in recounting the story. In Paul Auster's book *City of Glass* the main character is called Quinn. He writes detective novels under the pseudonym William Wilson. His private investigator and narrator is called Max Work. In discussing this relationship Auster writes:

> In the triad of selves that Quinn had become, Wilson served as a kind of ventriloquist. Quinn himself was the dummy, and Work was the animated voice that gave purpose to the enterprise. If Wilson was an illusion, he nevertheless justified the lives of the other two. If Wilson did not exist, he nevertheless was the bridge that allowed Quinn to pass from himself into Work. And little by little, Work had become a presence in Quinn's life, his interior brother, his comrade in solitude. pp.11–12.

A little later, the telephone rings. 'Who is this?' 'Is this Paul Auster?' asked the voice. 'I would like to speak to Mr. Paul Auster.' 'There's no one here by that name.'

Not only is the real author excluded (though later included when Quinn pretends to be an employee of the

Auster Detective Agency) but the author Quinn decentres himself to become Wilson, whose key character, the symbolically named Work, is the real animating force of the activity of producing his fiction. Is the author less visible, doubly reduced to the will of a fictional character, or more visible in his self-consciousness?

Just before this incident Quinn has been reading Marco Polo's *Travels*, the first page of which states:

> We will set down things seen as seen, things heard as heard, so that our book may be an accurate record, free from any sort of fabrication. And all who read this book or hear it may do so with full conscience, because it contains nothing but the truth. Just as Quinn was beginning to ponder the meaning of the sentences, to turn their crisp assurances over in his mind, the telephone rang. p.12.

Here is the questioning of the 'mirror of nature' view of philosophy, history, geographical writing that the post-modern critique takes as the basis for its languages games. Marco Polo also crops up in Italo Calvino's novel *Invisible Cities* as a character who is both fictional and historical. This ambiguity derives from the ironic reading of Marco Polo's certainty that he was representing reality. In Calvino's novel he is only knowable from the texts he wrote and those written about him. These, and Calvino's imaginative fiction, itself partly constructed on Polo's reported travels, create the character.

But *Invisible Cities* signifies not only a questioning of the capacity of the author to represent reality, it questions the binary, either/or way of thinking characteristic of the modernist perception of space and the place of the subject as an observer from a privileged perspective, or centre. Marco Polo is requested by Kubla Khan to describe the cities of his empire. The Great Khan's empire includes such cities as Penthesilia which sprawls in an unbounded suburban mass with no clear focus, Cecilia which spreads out extensively over space, and Tonde which covers the whole world. These impossible cities break all the rules of representation until we see that they are symbols of different kinds of world. There is the space of the sacred and that of the profane, that of the dead and of the living, of illusion and reality. They are all, in Polo's impossible account, descriptions of different aspects of Venice. Brian McHale has noted how Calvino's cities echo Foucault's idea of *heterotopia*, a space which makes the drawing of definite boundaries, centres and regularities impossible. It is not capable of conceptualization in binary terms, it is both/and rather than either/or. This is the space of paradox, which truly undermines modernist methods of reasoning, even undermines language itself by making specific naming of places in space impossible.

This is reminiscent of Thomas Pynchon's account of Germany immediately after defeat by the allies in *Gravity's Rainbow*, often taken as the exemplar of postmodern writing. Boundaries have disappeared, there are great migrations of refugees, a struggle by the occupying powers to dominate this space, illegal activity is legal, abnormality is normal. Into this world enters Pynchon's world of illusion, the mass media from which he draws metaphors which are hard to distinguish from 'reality' as represented in the fiction. This space is, thus, another example of plural worlds, and one which is also founded on the demise of an ordered system. Systems, with their controlling centres, exaggerated to the fullest extent in Nazi Germany, but also in the invading armies, are sinister but vulnerable to being undermined, at least in fiction.

The issues of fragmentation, anarchy, the undermining of modernist perspective, centredness and purpose are what give shape to the poetics of postmodern writing. Moreover, it is in the sphere of fiction that the idea of thinking the margins, of welcoming the margins of modernity as an active force for questioning the assumed privileging of western discourse, has gone furthest. Thus, the novels of

Gabriel García Marquéz, Carlos Fuentes and Salman Rushdie from 'the third world' or, even more strikingly, women writers, who write about gender-subordinated and/or ethnic minority situations, such as Maxime Hong Kingston, Alice Walker, Angela Carter or Toni Morrison, have 'democratized' fiction beyond its male, western stereotype. Amongst other things these writers problematize the division between the novel and history (Rushdie, García Marquéz, Fuentes), the novel and autobiography (Kingston, Walker), the novel and anthropology (Carter, Kingston) and the novel and psychology (Walker, Morrison).

To the extent that these writers problematize their subject-matter they can be seen as engaged in indirect practices of political subversion. Each, and many others who are included in the canon of postmodern fiction writers, has this in common amongst their many differences. To that extent, then, they clearly share much in common with the general project of modernity. By specifying the nature of marginal experience, pointing ironically to the ways that a supposedly emancipatory modernity marginalized so much of the diversity of subjected existence in its effort to focus its critique upon the limitations of pre-modern elitism, such authors move the modern project forward. The questions they pose are often politically unanswerable without recognizing the legitimacy of their claims. So the question of whether postmodern fiction has somehow left modernity behind is really the wrong question.

Postmodern fiction, like postmodern philosophy, lives to a large extent off the beast it attacks. The position of postmodern fiction is thus both within and ahead of modern fiction and many of the assumptions that have informed aesthetic and philosophical modernism. As Linda Hutcheon has put it:

the 'Post Position' signals its contradictory dependence on and independence from that which temporally preceded it and which literally made it possible. Postmodernism's

relation to modernism is, therefore, typically contradictory. . . It marks neither a simple and radical break
from it nor a straightforward continuity with it: it is both
and neither. And this would be the case in aesthetic,
philosophical, or ideological terms (Hutcheon 1988, p.18).

Despite this, it has to be said that much postmodern fiction,
in ambiguously maintaining its links while apparently
breaking its chains, leaves itself open to criticism.

Some of these criticisms will be dealt with in more detail
in the final section of this chapter. For the moment,
however, it may be noted that the elements of parody,
irony, play and experimental mind games to which it is
prone, leave it open to the question of how serious much of
it is. Added to which its tendency towards inward reflection
on the status of the author as a subject her or himself, rather
than a more direct attack on the institutional basis for the
situation that causes that problematization, often looks like
mere navel-contemplation. Some postmodern fiction, moreover, is negatively apocalyptic, seeing the displacement of
the self as the irresistible product of the systematization of
life through the mass media amongst other things. Treating
the institutions of mass culture as illusions into which fiction
escapes is ultimately quietistic. One response could be that
'it's only fiction'. But is it?

This lack of a project, other than critique, weakens the
creative, progressive thematics which postmodern fiction
has raised for consideration. Of particular importance is its
revaluation of specifically local motifs which continue, not as
residues from some pre-modern inheritance such as community, but rather as a set of resistances to the homogenizing,
monolithic assumptions of modernity. This is a potentially
crucial aspect of the subverting tendency within postmodernism. The recognition of difference, struggling to
prevent its absorption into a systematized whole, whether
mass culture, mass production or the mass media, could be
one of the more valuable products of postmodernism's effort

to deconstruct the master institutions of modernity. This is where it connects with the insights which have emerged simultaneously from postmodern philosophy. The connection centres on the idea that dominant discourses are time and space specific, and that to alter them they have first to be fragmented, then the pluralized voices that challenged them have to speak to each other to reconstruct a new kind of more democratized, less monolithic discourse, or set of discourses, concerning both thought and action.

Postmodern architecture

It was in the urban landscapes of large American and European cities that postmodernism first imprinted itself upon the gaze of the ordinary public. In the late 1970s new styles of architecture appeared, apparently rejecting the austerity of modernism by including ornamentation, colour (of a pastel rather than a primary kind) and heterogeneous forms such as the barrel-vaulted glass atrium or the classical facade with pitched roof, in place of the uniform cubes of late modernism. By the late 1980s postmodern architecture consisted of a number of different styles, some of which could even be seen to be obvious continuations of modernism, notably the 'high-tech' buildings of Norman Foster, especially his Hong Kong & Shanghai Bank, and Richard Rogers, whose Lloyds Insurance building in the City of London celebrated, as did Foster's, the modernist idea that function should not only determine form but that it should pervade its every visible facet.

Other architects whose work has been described as postmodern, such as Charles Moore, Michael Graves, Helmut Jahn, Leon Krier, Ricardo Bofill, Aldo Rossi and the later designs of Philip Johnson, amongst many, have rejected Mies van der Rohe's thesis that 'Less is more', the clarion call of modernism, and decided that pure form is not enough. Rossi and Krier's work has been described as 'neorationalist', Moore's and Bofill's as 'neoclassicist', Graves' and Johnson's as 'historicist', while Jahn's glass and steel towers both echo modernist uses of material and the revival of typical early modern American skyscraper forms, themselves often neogothic in inspiration. It is strange, therefore, that criticism has frequently been directed at postmodern architecture because of its lack of aesthetic reference to historical forms of building and design. It is said, particularly by Frederic Jameson (to whose critique I will return in the final section of this chapter) that postmodern architecture is merely pastiche, playful, not serious, populist, and marks a departure from the higher ideals to which modernism, through its aesthetic connections with the theory of proportion in classical architecture, aspired. This criticism, it is worth adding, has also been made of postmodern fiction, by Charles Newman and others, though as we have seen, it hardly stands close scrutiny given the often grand historical sweep which such texts as those of García Marquéz, Rushdie and Calvino display.

Nevertheless, it is a charge worth exploring, since it is clear that the way historical reference is incorporated in postmodern architecture is very different from that represented in modernist stylistics. Perhaps the key characteristics of postmodern architecture, consistent with the other postmodernist themes under discussion, is that it is 'double-coded'. Whereas modernist architecture communicated with the past and present by means of a code that was hermetically sealed to all who were not privileged members of the professional elite who could be expected to know or understand what was going on, postmodern architecture both does that same thing, in a more obvious and specific way, and communicates directly, often with local relevance, to the ordinary public who live with its results. In this sense postmodern architecture can often be irreverent in the way that it uses and combines motifs from the past. Such ironies are equally meant to appeal to the public and professional audience alike. This is where postmodernism differs significantly from the po-faced anti-modernism of Quinlan Terry and the Prince of Wales. Their classicism is undiluted revivalism intended to be revered as much as enjoyed.

We can explore the historical dimension in three sub-planes through examining three instances of postmodern architecture that range from the macro to the micro scales. The first example is Ricardo Bofill's monumental constructions as exemplified in the French new town of St-Quentin-en-Yvelines near Paris and in the mediterranean city of Montpellier (see Plate 4). Both are large-scale public sector housing schemes, a fact which marks Bofill's work thus far as somewhat distinct from the office buildings or museums of which much postmodern architecture seems presently to consist. Bofill builds high-rise architecture of a scale more typical of the late modernist housing schemes which pioneered the style. However, the design of the schemes themselves seems to owe more to Cecil B. de Mille or at least Caesar's Rome, than to Le Corbusier. In St-Quentin the monumental slabs are set in a lake and either side of the apartment windows are set series of gigantic classical pillars, much greater in scale than those ever built in Athens, Rome or even nineteenth-century New York, Paris or London.

In Montpellier, the same monumental style is repeated except on a more limited scale. The Antigone, as his development is named, flows from the modernist Polygone retail and office centre located at the open end of what has been turned into a vast, *fin de siècle* piazza complete with revivalist fountain and refurbished opera house. Antigone itself consists of two large, circular piazzas, linked by a 'neck' from the side of which entry is made into the vast enclosed spaces. Again, the housing is multi-storey and the main projecting points where curve meets line are set off by the enormous classical pillars. Within the piazzas, separating off pedestrianized circulation space from relaxation space are pedimented arches, more decorative than functional. The whole edifice is built of golden, prefabricated cement panels redolent in colour and texture of Cotswold stone.

Bofill's designs are slightly unnerving in that they can at first seem to echo the architecture of less elevated historical episodes such as Mussolini's Rome. But there is less quasi-modern stylization, and more, albeit prefabricated, attention to social enclosure than triumphalism in the architecture. The buildings convey a sense both of providing secure, pleasant, traffic-free living space and of an ironic representation of the particular local history of these French cities as parts of the Romanized empire. Moreover, by providing such palatial-looking accommodation (inside, the apartments are cramped functional-modern) for public sector tenants the point is made that in the contemporary period there is no need for palaces only to be associated with the luxury housing of the rich. That class transgression and the care with which the open space, shopping and drinking amenities have been incorporated into the overall design suggest an, albeit idiosyncratic, improvement on the alienating products of modernist mass housing policy.

Philip Johnson's AT&T Building in Manhattan is also typically monumental, though in this case a single tower. Johnson, who was a disciple of Le Corbusier, has adapted his late modernist steel and glass cubism by changing the facing material to the postmodernist pastel of polished pink granite, then topping the whole edifice off with a Chippendale broken pediment. This joke, for it is too blatant an act to be considered irony or even parody, has caused outrage because of its apparent meaninglessness and egotism. But it deflects attention from two more positive features of postmodernism. First, it lessens the distance, at least symbolically, between the higher reaches of aesthetic professionalism and the man or woman in the street, each of whom may reflect on the similarity between the building and the tallboy in auntie's bedroom. But secondly, and more importantly, the design incorporates a public plaza which invites the passer-by into the building, to treat it, if only during the working day, as a space for sociability, unlike its modernist forebears. Foster's bank building in Hong Kong does the same in opening up a shared space through which the public is encouraged to pass to a nearby park. Is this just corporate capitalism pretending to be friendly? Perhaps. But in the process a little of the alienation created by modernist exclusiveness is undermined.

The micro-scale example of postmodern historicity is Charles Moore's Piazza d'Italia in New Orleans. This is precisely a local cultural artefact in that it is simply an open public arena on a small scale built in and for the Italian community in the city. It is a circular piazza, set in the grid of a streetblock, surrounded by various motifs from the distant and not so distant past. Classical arches, a podium, Latin inscriptions, a Fontana de Trevi and black and white contrasts are reminiscent of the Gothic Duomo of Florence or Siena. Because the Italian community of the city is predominantly Sicilian in origin the concentric circles of the piazza are transected by a map of Italy with Sicily in the centre. There is illusion where a column turns into a fountain, and in the use of materials which, despite appearances, are mass produced cement and steel, and the ornamentation has the look not of the craftsman's effort but of the factory-produced artefact. Despite its obviousness, or more likely because of it, the construction works and is locally popular through its capacity to echo and reproduce in a new-old form the local identity of those uprooted by the global forces of modernity. Once again the style is inclusive, democratic and historicist, but in ways that have meaning for the residents of the locality.

These themes also underlie the architectural philosophies of the neo-rationalists Aldo Rossi and Leon Krier. They have reacted against Le Corbusier's injuction to 'kill the street' by rethinking the elements of the pre-modern city, destroyed under the modernist regime, in terms of basic forms and functions. The street, the open space and the different types of buildings, domestic, official, commercial and so on constitute the elements which they have sought to reintegrate. This reworking of classical motifs has led Krier to design schemes which link functions such as the public and the private through reviving the street, the square, the monumental focusing point. Designs for private or public housing include the street, not necessarily as a grid-like dividing device but a diagonal, integrating space of flows in layouts which respect human scale. There is, in this architecture, some danger of tipping over into reactionary anti-modernism but thus far this pitfall seems to have been avoided, not least by the measure of irony and parody of the past which their designs continue to display.

Sometimes the ironic playfulness of postmodern architecture tips over in the other direction, back to a new kind of elitism. This is a danger which Michael Graves seems to have flirted with unsuccessfully. As Linda Hutcheon puts it in discussing his (unbuilt) amber, turquoise and magenta Fargo-Moorhead Cultural Bridge between North Dakota and Minnesota, drawing on the analysis of the architectural historian Charles Jencks:

> Jencks has trouble dealing . . . with its admitted echoes of Ledoux, Castle Howard, Serharia, Wilson's architecture at Kew, Asplund, Borromini and others . . . of modernist concrete construction, of mannerist broken pediments, and of cubist colours. Jencks acknowledges that the meaning of these historical references would likely be lost on the average citizen of the American mid-west. (Hutcheon 1988, p.34).

This seems to be an example of the architect's wish to display his learning to the profession, and also outperform his previous masterpieces (as at Portland, Oregon, in the chocolate-box of a public facilities building, decorated with a bronze bust of 'Portlandia', second only in scale to the Statue of Liberty), rather than speak democratically to the local citizenry.

So, postmodernism in architecture is as prone as postmodern fiction to the dangers of incomprehensibility, but neither at their best suffer from this problem as much as the avowedly elitist products of hermetic late modernism. Postmodernism as built form is conscious of the need to close the gap between high and low culture, to communicate in symbols which the untutored citizen may be better able to understand and enjoy, and, above all, to replace the monolithic, homogeneous universality of modernist discourse with a more heterogeneous, locally sensitive and inclusive language which entertains as it parodies the pretensions of the past.

The critique of postmodernism

Perhaps surprisingly, given what has been said about the elements of subversion, irreverence, parody and sensitivity to locality, even a degree of popular democracy, that are contained within the postmodern critique, it has received its sternest criticisms from Marxist aestheticians. The foremost among these has been Frederic Jameson. Jameson sees postmodernism in all its forms; poetry, fiction, architecture, music and the visual arts, as the cultural correlate of the latest stage in the development of capitalism, the capitalism of pure consumption, the onset of consumer society. This society is advanced, hyper-modern, postindustrial, media-dominated, given to indulging in spectacle, dominated by multinational capital. Its two most significant features are its preference for pastiche and a schizophrenic disposition.

By pastiche, Jameson means the taking of original styles and imitating or mimicking them in the absence of some sense of respect for them. Pastiche, Jameson says, is humourless because it has lost touch with the universal norms by means of which artists or satirists justify picking upon particular styles to ridicule. In the modernist era there were such norms, even though the styles could be diverse and original. But because of that originality, which also conveyed a sense of authenticity, the satirist remained in touch with the norms by which the judgement of authenticity

109

had been made. Amongst the most important of such norms was the concept of the authentic, creative individual. Pastiche signifies that individualism of that kind is dead for the reasons that have been discussed already. The critique of subjectivity as produced by Foucault; the idea that only texts matter (and are in any case the product of many texts shimmering off each other, after Derrida); and the apocalyptic notion of the death of the subject proposed by those, such as Jean Baudrillard, who see us all as slaves to the power of mass-media – all these have contributed to a strange devaluing of the subject, in which condition pastiche thrives.

Moreover, as Jameson puts it, in seeking to explain the emergence of pastiche as a kind of sub-aesthetic:

> There is another sense in which the writers and artists of the present day will no longer be able to invent new styles and worlds – they've already been invented; only a limited number of combinations are possible; the most unique ones have been thought of already. So the weight of the whole modernist aesthetic tradition – now dead – also 'weighs like a nightmare on the brains of the living,' as Marx said in another context (Jameson 1985, p.115).

So art becomes artifice, the endless recycling of the styles of the past. Hence, the inflated market for nostalgia and the reinterpretation of the past in fiction, film, art and architecture, even in rock music, once the province of a kind of insurgent originality. Old plots, like old songs or themes, are plagiarized unashamedly, given an archaic feel even when the setting may be a contemporary one. Consumer capitalism seems to have robbed contemporary culture of the capacity to produce original statements. Worse than that, its artefacts confine us, exclude us, disorient us as in the examples Jameson gives of the postmodern hotels and shopping plazas which resist decoding, save only to project an image of mindless consumption upon our brains.

The schizophrenic aspect that Jameson sees in post-modernism derives from what he calls the disappearance of a sense of history. The cultural recycling places us in a permanent present of changing images supplied by the mass-media, the fashion industry, advertising, changes in style. This is something akin to the experience of the schizophrenic patient who suffers a loss of the integrated view of the self as having a past, present and future, and a sense of detachment from reality.

Because of this fragmentation of time, exemplified in the pervasiveness of such ideas as 'built-in obsolescence' and 'replacement buying' which the communications industries project as the motive force of consumer society, its members begin to experience a kind of historical amnesia. We forget the past and accept its reproduction in various pre-packaged forms of nostalgia. In that process lies the danger – Jameson leaves his options open at this point – that postmodernism means passive compliance with this dominating consumer society. Unlike modernism which produced culturally dissonant, even shocking subversions of and oppositions to the norms of conventional bourgeois society, postmodernism, for Jameson, lacks this sense of resistance.

To some extent, these arguments have been anticipated in the preceding discussion. It is important, as was noted in the assessment of postmodernist fiction and architecture, to recognize that there is some basis for Jameson's strictures. Postmodernism can seem, as Jameson and others have said elsewhere, depthless, eclectic and disoriented. Moreover, in architecture especially, it seems highly complicit with the power structure of consumer society. Unquestionably, many postmodern buildings and even wider segments of the urban landscape such as the waterfront developments that have become commonplace in large cities, cater to the tastes and lifestyles of the rich and famous. Corporate capital was amongst the earliest purchasers of the fashionably new styles. And although it is important not to overlook the role of the public sector in commissioning the work of some of the leading newer architects such as Bofill, Graves, Moore and Krier, it can still, as a critic in the *Architectural Review* put it, 'look like little more than the pretty plaything of rampant capitalism'.

It is not clear why this should surprise the critics. Corporate capital quickly appropriated virtually every fashionable new architectural style that preceded postmodern architecture. It is difficult to see why postmodernism should be any different. In this respect it can be argued that these styles are no more or less complicit with the values of the corporate elite than any other.

But, to return to the issue Jameson raises regarding the pastiche-like quality of postmodern aesthetic forms, it is instructive to consider the distinction he makes between parody (good) and pastiche (bad). In a lengthy discussion of the concept of parody Linda Hutcheon argues that its meaning is more ambiguous than Jameson allows. While he defines it solely as satirical or ridiculing imitation she points out that the root of the word in the Greek *para* gives it the double meaning both of 'against' and also 'beside'. On this basis postmodernism is engaged in parody rather than pastiche because it involves critical, often ironic reinterpretation of standard aesthetic norms, pointing to differences but remaining within or beside the tradition. One of the more common ironic references is towards modernism's loss of touch with the local and popular levels of aesthetic appreciation.

The other dimension of Jameson's critique – namely that postmodernism marks a loss of historical reference, a schizophrenic problem of identity in relation to time, a situation of time being a permanently recycled sense of the present – seems equally unfounded when consideration is given to the way that historical reference infuses large areas of postmodern aesthetics. Moreover, if the second meaning of the concept of parody is deployed it is much harder to argue as Jameson does that postmodernism represents a kind of neutral, untethered relationship to the canon of norms or aesthetic regime that developed with modernism's challenge to classical aesthetics. There are striking similarities between modernism's Janus-face, looking backwards in order to move forward, and that of postmodernism in which there is, if anything, a stronger desire to vault backwards over the austere hermeticism of the late modern era in order to move forward into a renewed, more accessible aesthetic regime.

In conclusion, therefore, these two main critical thrusts, around which other critical charges have accreted, are overexaggerated. They fail to recognize the ambiguity in postmodern art and architecture between working within the cultural and wider socio-economic system and simultaneously subverting aspects of it. Irony is mistaken for oppositionism, and local sensitivity – where it exists – for a rejection of universal and transcendent norms. Even Jameson does not deny the possibility that progressive cultural and social insights and practices can arise from within the postmodern perspective. Perhaps undue attention has been paid to postmodernism's historical coincidence with the rise of neoconservative politics and the crisis of progressive institutions such as the Keynesian welfare state and Fordist modes of regulation and forms of accumulation. The undoubted reductionism in Jameson's analysis – shared with other Marxist critiques such as that of Terry Eagleton, Mike Davis and others whose thoughtful commentaries have appeared in the *New Left Review* during the 1980s – is testimony to the problems of engaging in a totalizing form of modern discourse. Postmodernism's own critique questions precisely the monolithic, totalizing perspective.

CHAPTER FIVE

Locality and social innovation

Localism versus centralism

Amongst the concepts that the postmodern critique of modernist theory consistently registers is the *local* dimension of thought and action. Local discourses tend to be privileged by Foucault for their capacity to disclose the microstructures of the operation of power relations. Local narrative is highlighted by Lyotard because it problematizes the unjustifiable grand, universalizing narratives of modern philophical method and modes of defining reason. Rorty, too, rejects the monolithic 'mirror of nature' theory of knowledge characteristic of modern philosophy. He makes the case for a more pragmatic way of arriving at agreed truth through dialogue between persons bringing their local interpretations to the debating and adjudicating forum in a quest for solidarity rather than a spurious objectivity. Unger draws our attention to the idea of justice as a pluralistic concern of individuals and local movements committed to a responsive rather than a deterministic form of jurisprudence. Postmodern writers stress in ironic ways the claims of local or particular narratives that have beeen excluded from the mainstream as merely marginal and belonging to the category of 'the other'. And postmodern arhitecture seeks to restore identity to local cultures swamped hitherto by the austere universalism of modernist aesthetics. Local sensitivity, the use of vernacular forms and the reinterpretation of

Plate 1 Nineteenth century Manchester

Plate 2 Test track for Fiat vehicles on the roof of the Lingotto workshops, 1936

Plate 3 Rouge River Ford complex.

Plate 4 'Antigone': Ricardo Bofill's housing scheme at Montpellier.

the past in ways which give local meaning to the present are part of that project.

There is, therefore, a remarkable unanimity amongst such thinkers and schools of thought that the local dimension has been for too long neglected by an overcentralized, dominating and exclusive modernist culture. Contemporary social innovation shifts the pivot of creativity from top down to bottom up. Social innovation covers a wide range of aesthetic, moral and practical activity. It is the characteristic source of the dynamism of modernity. Much of that dynamism came from centralizing forces such as the modern corporation, as in the case of flow-line assembly in industry; the state with its Keynesian regulatory innovations of demand management and welfare provision; and the academy, with its absorption and retransmission of standardized modernist aesthetic norms. But the successful practices of even the most powerful western corporations have been challenged and undermined by those of innovative newcomers from the Far East. The state has in many cases diminished, and in others significantly revised its regulatory functions towards corporate affairs. And the growing internationalization of economic regulation, visible clearly in the Europe of an open market, but also in the ramifying networks of global economic power, further weakens the economic purchase that can be brought to bear by the individual modern nation-state upon matters of production, distribution and trade. In the cultural sphere, difference rather that homogeneity is widely celebrated as aesthetic standards become more cosmopolitan.

As the will and capacity of the state to solve widespread problems of unemployment, social malaise and even political discontent, come into question, a greater responsibility – though not necessarily a greater degree of power – devolves upon the locality. Even in some of the less neoconservatively governed countries such as the welfare democracies of Scandinavia and the Netherlands, the allocation of welfare, though not the determination of overall budgets, is becoming

115

an increasingly localized function. In France, traditionally the most centralized of modern nation-states, responsibilities have been decentralized to local municipal as well as regional levels of government. Britain seems to be the clear exception to this tendency. Far from increasing the degree of responsibility for welfare and other services such as housing and education provision at the local level, the government has, for the ten-year period after 1979, been curbing powers, limiting revenue-raising capacity and, in some cases, dismantling the machinery of local government, notably the metropolitan county councils. In place of hitherto locally determined standards of provision, the central state has set in place a number of indicative controls on the levels of revenue raising and local expenditure, it has relaxed planning controls over some parts of cities to enable development to take place in enterprise zones, and in other parts replaced the local planning apparatus with urban development corporations charged with revitalizing rundown waterfront and other deindustrialized areas. Such policies are a reaction against what was perceived as an overaccumulation of fiscal and political power at local level.

These examples of British exceptionalism pose interesting questions in the context of the contemporary critique of modernity. Does Thatcherism signify a strand of reactionary anti-modernism comparable to that represented in the attacks upon modern architecture from the Prince of Wales? Or does it point to a return to the doctrines associated with the theory which underpinned the early modern nation-state with its stress on sovereignty, individual freedom and the authority of the rule of law? Is Thatcherism not so much a reaction against modernity in general as against the institutional forms it took in the late modern period typified by a Keynesian approach to economic management and a wide-ranging set of social provisions through the welfare state? Is it, in other words, a reaction against the Fordist regime of accumulation and mode of regulation?

It is possible to give a positive answer to all of these

questions. The weaker case for a positive answer lies in the aesthetic sphere. It is not clear that Thatcherism contains aesthetic principles except to revere those works of art that have a high market value. The attempt in 1988 to attract the Thyssen collection to Britain by suddenly finding the hundreds of millions of pounds necessary to acquire it while at the same time cutting the budget for state-funding of the arts, a decision which has had negative consequences for local aesthetic innovation, would be indicative of that disposition. Moreover, the general policy of encouraging business corporations to finance an increasing proportion of the arts budget, and changes being made to the legal responsibilities of museums to enable them to sell off their less popular exhibits, both point in the direction of what might be called the colonization of aesthetics by the market place. From being the repository of culture the museum becomes its trade centre.

The grounds for a positive answer improve if we conceive of Thatcherism as signifying a reassertion of the values of state sovereignty, individual freedom and the rule of law, an early modern framework reinterpreted through the principle of market exchange as the essential individual right to choose. Even the death of community seems to have been incorporated in the Thatcherian claim that there is no such thing as society, only individuals and families. To some extent Unger's thesis that modernity's fundamental principle of justice is freedom of contract to protect the money-making ethic gains support from observation of the practices of neoconservative governments. Thus, the individual right to buy housing, health care, education and company equity has been elevated far above the idea of the citizen's right to receive communal provision of social and other welfare services. In the process, the local, democratically controlled councils that provide such services are undermined by central state authority, or self-destruct under local neo-conservative regimes.

This line of reasoning gains overwhelming support in the

light of the proposition that the New Right doctrine is fundamentally opposed to the regulatory regimes typical of later modernity. Keynesianism is particularly vilified by neoconservatives for its feather-bedding of the social and economic casualties of modernity and, worst of all, its perceived tendency to devalue the medium and measure of exchange through inflation. Monetarism has been used to choke off inflation, though in both the UK and the USA quasi-Keynesian instruments such as defence expenditure and the unleashing of consumption booms have been deployed, the rhetoric notwithstanding. In parallel, the institutions and principles of the welfare state have been subjected to swingeing criticisms and the threat of being dismantled. This is partly because of what is perceived as their 'crowding out' of entrepreneurial scope by absorbing large amounts of public expenditure (hence also, it is proposed, further fuel for inflation), partly because of their perceived tendency to create a 'dependency' rather than an invigorating 'enterprise' culture. Moreover, the ideals of professional service and the satisfaction of needs are considered anathema to an ideology committed to the principle of 'value for money'.

Finally, even elements of Fordism other than those mentioned have been under attack. The monopoly powers of large, multinational corporations have been curbed by the rhetoric and policies of stimulating competition. But it is what are perceived as the monopoly powers of labour that have been subject to the stronger controls in Britain. The institutional structures of collective bargaining have been weakened by legislation circumscribing the traditional rights of trades unions to manage their affairs as they consider fit. In concert with an assault by larger corporations on the concept of national wage agreements, this has led to more locally based bargaining and the emergence of geographical differences in UK rates of pay in services such as health care, communications and, possibly in future, education as well as industries such as steel, engineering and printing.

Thus we see in neoconservative politics the attempt to resolve the fundamental contradiction of modernity between the desire to secure the rights of the individual citizen to autonomy and liberty and the desire that such rights should be realized within an ordered, centrally powerful sovereign state. The contradiction is being reconciled by a redefinition of citizenship which emphasizes market rights over social, political, welfare and even civil rights. This is clearly a dangerously reductionist approach to take in societies informed by a democratic consciousness of past struggles to establish precisely those non-market citizenship rights which are, in the British case, being eroded daily. This chapter will explore the prospects for a re-exertion of citizenship claims, paying special attention to the role of local discourse, initiatives and movements in the context of a growing unevenness in the distribution over urban and regional space of access to even the growing range of market rights, let alone other more collectively expressed rights.

Locality in a polarizing society

To a large extent the social, cultural and political changes that heralded the era of modernity and have signalled momentous developments within it, have been stimulated by shifts occurring in the economy – more accurately the political economy – though such changes cannot simply be reduced to a mirror-like reflection of economic upheavals. A major study of the impact upon Britain's urban and regional system of economic restructuring triggered by the crisis of Fordism has revealed, amongst other things, the quite dramatic reversals of fortune experienced by diverse social groups, depending upon the locality in which they live and work.

British society, largely an urbanized one, has been experiencing significant polarization between the affluent and the indigent, and between its different cities and

119

regions. Yet one of the most instructive findings has been the manner in which local social innovation had played a part either in enabling fortuitously located places to anticipate and prepare for change, thus giving their residents a competitive edge, or had been a response to economic setbacks, enabling dislocated communities to come to terms with local crises. This element of local capacity, not necessarily a reactive but a proactive disposition, is not equally shared. Some localities lose that capacity with economic reversal, some otherwise favourably located in a growth area may be late in waking up to the need for change. But it seems that, even in the face of increasingly centralizing powers of state control, local initiative can still be found. Importantly, where local self-help or initiative-taking is found, it seldom draws on older traditions of authority such as one would expect to find in long-established communities. Rather, it arises from the struggles by individuals and organizations, both formal and informal, to press local claims for justice and prosperity but also, presumably, exclusivity, privilege and a larger, not simply a fairer, share of the cake. A fuller report of the findings can be found in a book entitled *Localities* edited by this author. The following pages of this section provide a summary and a prelude to a discussion of the meaning and importance of locality in the face of a contemporary grand narrative of state sovereignty and market hegemony.

The study selected seven very different localities for investigation: towns and areas of cities in the depressed north and the booming south of England; localities that were closely linked to Fordist-type industry such as the Speke, Halewood and Kirkby areas of Liverpool, Longbridge and Bournville in Birmingham, and Middlesbrough; localities that were experiencing growth in financial services and high technology industry such as Cheltenham and Swindon; and localities that had experienced reversals in established production industries and older services like tourism in Lancaster and Morecambe, Margate, Ramsgate and

Broadstairs – the last three now known as the Isle of Thanet. Each of these localities has experienced the transformations of modernity in differing ways, at differing times and to differing degrees. But one thing that has been common to them is that they have all been increasingly influenced by the impact of discourses emanating from and decisions made in London.

London was, as it remains, the city that serviced world trade and finance, a global centre for luxury consumption, a city to which modern industry came surprisingly late and from which much of it left rather early. For a significant period, though, concentrated either side of the midpoint of the twentieth century, around the beginning of the late modern period while London was seeking a post-imperial role, its importance for the localities and regions over which its institutions ruled can hardly be overestimated.

As Fordism and the Keynesian welfare state developed, the intervention of centrally situated institutions in the everyday life of business and locality grew immensely. The growth of monopoly within the corporate sector, and the weakening of industries located in the growth centres of the early modern period, meant that ownership of regional industry became centralized. Welfare spending, including the further redirection of employment to those now declining cities and regions, became a structural element of the United Kingdom's economy. The advent of London-centred radio and television programming created a new relation of cultural dominance and dependence between the capital and 'the provinces'. However, as a result of that closer integration between the two, differences in levels of prosperity between London, its surrounding region and the more impoverished parts of the country began slowly to lessen. Unemployment differentials which in 1931 were enormous between the south east at 7.8 per cent and the northern regions of England at 19.2 per cent had moderated equally significantly to 2.2 and 3.8 per cent respectively by 1961. Income inequality between the classes, which as late as 1954 showed the after-tax income of the top 10 per cent at well above double that of the lowest 30 per cent of earners, had slowly narrowed such that it was marginally less than double by 1974. Each of these important moves towards greater equality within and across the United Kingdom was a result, in large part, of the greater integration of central decision making located in London into concern for the condition of the rest of the urban and regional system over which it wielded increasing economic and political power.

As British society looked more inwardly at its own problems, so the tremendous financial and governmental power of the centre began to reorganize in halting and complex ways the open space economy of the sovereign kingdom. Loss of regional control meant that business decisions were increasingly taken centrally. To some extent these could be integrated with political decisions to 'modernize' the urban fabric and social horizons of the country. A city such as Liverpool which in the 1930s had had to petition Parliament to acquire the legislation to undertake its own urban renewal became in the 1950s and 1960s almost a laboratory for social democratic planning. National and international business was induced to locate Fordist industry such as car production on the outskirts of the city where state-subsidized council housing was constructed on a mass scale to house the workers. By and large the work was semi-skilled, routine assembly with little managerial autonomy allowed to local executives. Elsewhere, nationalization and concentration of ownership in the private sector, linked to a growth-centre policy from government, could lead to the rapid restructuring and modernization of heavy industry in a town such as Middlesbrough with relatively little local control being exerted. Thus, the regional mosaic was transformed into an integrated hierarchical structure.

This spatial division of labour mimicked the Fordist hierarchy of the multinational corporations largely responsible for it: executives, finance specialists and research teams centred in or near London; design and production of manufactured goods embodying traditional craft skills in or near semi-peripheral conurbations such as Birmingham or Manchester; and assembly work for semi-skilled workers in the 'screwdriver factories' of the periphery. As one moved down this hierarchy so the proportion of women employed in production in such companies tended to increase, especially in such industries as electronics, clothing and food processing. Local and regional economies that had once been relatively integrated were increasingly turned inside out. Large corporations would habitually source necessary products from within their own organization, consisting typically of a series of increasingly globally distributed mass production units.

By the mid-1970s the great functional diversity of the cities and regions of the United Kingdom had been substantially evened out into a more homogeneous pattern. Three examples illustrate this. All large cities in the United Kingdom had, by the mid-1970s, a serious and accelerating 'inner-city problem'. Although complex, the causes could be traced to the loss of employment opportunities brought on by economic restructuring and the decentralization of work to modern, peripheral environments. Ethnic-minority populations came to be concentrated in areas vacated by the upwardly mobile. This combined with the decay of older housing stock for which it was often impossible to acquire private mortgage finance, and public sector redevelopment which often produced new housing expensive to service, sometimes poorly constructed and, if it was high-rise or deck-access, unpopular with consumers. Accordingly, inner cities everywhere became concentrations of the poorer, less qualified and socially stigmatized strata of the population. This crisis has normally been perceived as one only capable of management by central rather than local state initiative with the precise policy instruments shifting from plan to market and partnership to central control.

Secondly, most non-metropolitan towns showed signific-

123

ant growth in employment during the period when the inner-city crisis was developing. Between 1971 and 1981 Great Britain's inner cities lost 538 000 jobs while the small towns and rural areas increased their overall employment by 404 000. What is particularly remarkable is that this occurred during a period in which Great Britain lost 590 000 jobs. Northern Ireland actually gained 15 000 jobs, its 69 000 loss in manufacturing being compensated by services gains. Nor were these small-town jobs due to some revival of traditional rural activity, rather they were in the service sector, especially private services. However, it is worth noting that a process of 'rural industrialization' which had been most pronounced in the 1951–71 period came to a dramatic end with the loss of 717 000 manufacturing jobs in small towns and rural areas between 1971 and 1981. This was not far behind the job loss in cities. They accounted for 1.21 million of Great Britain's 1.93 million manufacturing job loss during the period. In percentage terms the rural rate was, at 17 per cent, just over half the urban rate of job loss of 33 per cent.

Thirdly, the United Kingdom has increasingly become a service economy, certainly from the employment viewpoint. Great Britain added 1.45 million service jobs to its labour market in the period 1971-81. Northern Ireland added 84 000 or 30 per cent to its service sector from 1971 to 1981. The only localities that lost service jobs were the inner cities. Elsewhere there was notable employment growth with very large numbers of jobs appearing in small-town and rural Britain. Where service sector growth occurred the emphasis was significantly greater in private than in public sector services. Hence, rural Britain gained 1.3 million service jobs of which two thirds were private sector; it was thus small town rural Britain which accounted for the lion's share of service sector employment growth in the 1970s, making the geographical and economic differences between urban and rural society even more blurred than hitherto.

Cities, then, were losing some of their aura, and with that their power, to smaller, more dynamic but less focused networks of workspace, residential space and leisure space. Such spaces could almost be described as problem-free for those gaining a niche within them. Property taxes would be low with relatively few public services, schools would probably be better than most inner-city schools, crime less prevalent, at least on the streets, and the air would be cleaner. This would be equally the case of the declining north as the booming south. The great countervailing tendency to deconcentration in northern cities was their higher general incidence of poverty, unemployment and low incomes.

The key factor driving southern prosperity in the contemporary urban and regional system is the vital international role played by London in the spheres of finance, banking, insurance, research, tourism, government, transportation, culture and private consumption, all of which are varieties of service activity. Moreover, such employment growth is spilling over to those smaller towns in rural settings to which attention has already been drawn. But these are overwhelmingly southern towns for the present. In this respect we can perceive the beneficial effects of internationalization upon specific localities. The restructuring process – moving towns away from reliance on agriculturally linked industries such as food-processing or fertilizers which, in a competitive international environment are becoming more and more capital-intensive, towards internationally integrated business, research or technology industries – is a relatively painless route to prosperity. But there is a more sombre side to the internationalization of economic linkages.

A great many of the UK localities that register the highest rates of long-term unemployment are those for which the efforts of local industry to restructure in the face of global competition came too late or not at all. Even those localities dependent on industries such as steel that were early to restructure profitably still had large numbers of workers on the unemployed lists more than five years after receiving their redundancy notices. In the bulk-steel producing localities, restructuring was forced upon the nationalized British Steel Corporation by a government insistent upon the need to be price competitive against the newer large-scale producers in Japan and the Third World, and quality competitive against established competititors closer to home in the EEC. The option of raising tariff barriers to protect an ailing industry had become politically and even institutionally unacceptable.

Looking at internationalization from a very different angle, combining employment and the culture of consumption in an age of increasing leisure, it is clear that localities that have played a traditional role as tourist resorts have been greatly disadvantaged by the rapid growth of the international package-holiday industry. While traditional seaside resorts lost as much as half their hotel and entertainments employment between 1971 and 1981, airport localities and business cities such as Heathrow, Aberdeen and Birmingham more than doubled theirs, as did the growing heritage centres such as Cheltenham and Warwick. Indeed almost everywhere in inland Britain registered an increase in employment in the hotel industry, while decline was confined mainly to the coast. There has, in other words, been a dramatic turning inside out of the tourism industry. International and national travel to and within the country is increasingly targeted on airport, business and heritage localities while travel to the sea is increasingly destined for overseas.

This shift in travel and tourism flows creates severe problems for the many traditional seaside resorts, already tempered by the seasonal nature of the hotel industry with its characteristically insecure and poorly paid employment. New or extended functions such as the conference trade or out-of-season breaks have been experimented with but there is strong competition for both from the inland heritage and business centres, and growing competition for the discretionary daytrip from new industrial heritage museums and theme parks. Unless seaside resorts can satisfactorily develop in those directions then the alternatives are decline and depopulation or the restructuring of their residential function to meet new needs. The presently expanding opportunities here are those services hitherto supplied directly by the welfare state such as nursing the elderly or providing accommodation for the homeless.

The change of government in 1979, breaking with the social democratic consensus that had been axiomatic since 1945, tilted the balance of social priorities away from preserving the fullest feasible extent of employment towards achieving the lowest feasible public expenditure and the fullest scope for private enterprise. Thus the requirement that a nationalized company such as the British Steel Corporation should reach profitability within five years from a loss position of nearly £2 billion placed enormous strains upon the corporation's internal labour market. A labour force of 197 000 in 1977 had been reduced to 52 000 by 1987, profitability had been achieved at £178 million, and the company was privatized in 1988. Such change inevitably impacts drastically upon specific localities dependent upon large steelworks for their livelihood. With the loss of the social and political cohesiveness supplied by the trades union movement in such localities goes the motive force for pressuring and negotiating with outside bodies through the local political system. Even in rather more diversified steel localities such as Middlesbrough 'local mafias' inevitably suffer a draining away of political strength even if slimdown as distinct from closure is their fate.

Alternatively, the intervention of the nation-state can unwittingly lead to the strengthening of local political resistance. Such a process has developed in Lancaster where a growth of public sector health and education employment has radicalized the local workforces, hitherto tending to be deferential from a long tradition of paternalism in the local linoleum industry. In Thanet, an example of the newly 'silent seaside', government policies of privatizing the care of the elderly and reducing the amount of council house building have created opportunities for local entrepreneurs to turn empty holiday accommodation into private nursing homes and bed-and-breakfast accommodation for homeless families, both funded – but now indirectly – by the state. Such overt signs of change have also alerted the hitherto individualistic and inward-looking political culture of the locality to the need for collective action through the local council to help revive the ailing tourist function of the resorts. A similar process seems to be beginning in Lancaster's neighbouring resort of Morecambe, similarly beset by changes in tourist taste.

Frequently, the intervention of the nation-state has had the most direct effects upon the fate of specific localities. Thus Cheltenham was the beneficiary of a major boost to its local labour and housing markets as a result of the expansion of government military expenditure in the 1980s. Both GCHQ, employing an estimated 10 000-plus, and local engineering companies closely tied to military aerospace have grown in size as employers. In the process the housing industry has been substantially boosted, retailing has expanded as new shopping centres designed to blend with Cheltenham's Regency heritage have been built, and the locally important private education system has itself shifted its emphasis from educating future civil servants to training potential captains of high technology industry.

The image of Cheltenham, consisting of its neoclassical facades, pump rooms, festival, Gold Cup and retired colonels could not be further removed from that of Swindon, an archetypal company town known for its railyards, locomotive engineering works, and its nodal role in Brunel's Great Western Railway. Yet those images belie a growing convergence of the two localities. Both have registered above-average growth in managerial and professional occupations for both men and women. Predictably, both have experienced high rates of growth in owner occupation of housing. Swindon (44 per cent) more than Cheltenham at the national average of 37 per cent. Finally, both showed exceptional increases in persons with degrees or equivalent qualifications with Cheltenham at 58 per cent ahead of Swindon's 50 per cent. By 1981 they were running neck and neck with 1057 and 1009 graduates or equivalent respectively.

Working-class Swindon has thus been moving upwards socially to meet formerly aristocratic Cheltenham halfway on a planned growth path. Cheltenham, though possessed of a substantial service sector, has now been overtaken even in financial services by Swindon. Both have benefited from government intervention but both also received decentralized finance and insurance offices from London when there were constraints on office development and sharp rent increases in the City. Swindon, in particular, benefits from its proximity to high-quality motorway, high-speed rail and international airport facilities. Swindon's boom is more pronounced than Cheltenham's because it has had more new economic activities to find as its old economic base contracted, hence its level of unemployment almost quadrupled in the early 1980s while Cheltenham's grew by less than half.

The changes in local life in these by no means untypical towns and cities have been dramatic. The crises of Fordism, Keynesianism and welfarism have been condensed by the shifts in policy at the level of the nation-state. With an open economy, a global function in financial services, and a growing heritage industry attracting an international clientele, Britain, in an era of the coming open European market, is going to be increasingly subject to the twists of fortune in the world economy. Through social power bases in business, government and culture, London exerts a significant, internally generated effectivity upon segments of the world economy, and increasingly looks outwards to the global scene. In the process there has been something of a turning away from more domestic concerns of welfare and social justice. In doing so the centre exerts a tightening regulatory grip on local affairs to free up opportunity for profitable private investment abroad. This has become an obstacle to social progress and a cause of social division and local discontent.

These processes are by no means confined to the case of London as a giant city in a relatively small national economy. Similar experiences are to be found in many American and European 'world cities' in relation to their hinterlands. In the American context the polarization of social classes is greater, in European cities less than in London. Either way, such developments are forcing smaller localities into a competition for jobs, investment and welfare expenditure. Moreover, the burden of responsibility for resolving problems is falling increasingly upon localities themselves.

Local potential and the status of 'locality'

Each of the localities portrayed in this polarizing, modernist, urban social system has displayed some capacity for proactivity built on locally established solidarities. The prospering localities of the south have displayed local effectivity in different ways. Cheltenham can afford to be relatively passive, offering a prestigious heritage backdrop of living and working conditions. But in the past, socially inclusive decisions to build substantial amounts of public housing and designate land for Fordist industry assisted its transition from an aristocratic watering hole to a modernized setting for development. Swindon has had, and continues, a more innovative tradition. When its early modern industrial base in railway engineering entered long-term decline, a coalition of labour organizations, small businessmen and local politicians were able to press the central state and Fordist engineering industry to expand housing and industry there, thus facilitating local restructuring. When in the 1970s the crisis of Fordism led to the decline of those industries too, the locality adjusted its strategy by presenting a new image to private capital in the booming financial services and high technology industries with results we have witnessed. Lancaster and Thanet, confronted with decline in their main tourism and production industries, have become more active. Lancaster was especially quick to recognize the small-business potential in its redundant linoleum and oilcloth mills, and this has made it one of the key activity centres for an innovative public–private partnership, Lancashire Enterprises Ltd, which now has a budget of over £10 million annually to invest in new businesses. Such initiative was partly stimulated by the changing labour market: as new public service employment replaced industry so the tradition of deference changed to one of resistance.

But there is also the experience of local innovation coming up against the limits of local power in the face of a hostile central state regime. Middlesbrough had during the Fordist era a strong local coalition of interests representing labour, industry and the municipality. By co-operating with sim-ilarly proactive neighbouring cities it was able to achieve substantial investment from government in large-scale industry, housing and infrastructure. But during the after-math of that interventionary era its coalition has been weakened by deindustrialization and its image stigmatized by the misfortune of the Cleveland child abuse case. A great deal of political and cultural rebuilding is required if this dislocated locality is to recover. That relatively little special attention is likely to be forthcoming from the centre is signified by Margaret Thatcher's reference to such localities as 'moaning minnies'.

The large cities of Birmingham and Liverpool resisted central government with innovatory policies based on local enterprise boards and locally sensitive housing construction. However, during an era when such local practices were perceived as a threat to the dominating pro-market ideology of the centre, these innovations could not be withstood and their councils and political initiators were swept away. In the case of Liverpool, the ideology of state sovereignty was a major theme, accepted by the parliamentary opposition as well as the government of the day, in justifying first the penalizing, then the removal of key political personnel in the local council. In the most socially deprived outer areas of Liverpool local innovation has been constrained to develop survival strategies in which local social networks have been responsible for establishing local welfare information centres, claimant's unions, housing co-operatives, credit unions and women's health action groups. Thus even in the most socially dislocated and politically constrained localities, social innovation survives in an attempt to limit the worst effects of social polarization, emigration and decline.

This strongly suggests that locality retains significance and social meaning in a contemporary period when the combined forces of modernity in the state, in multinational capital and in the mass media, have all but effaced the older social solidarities of community. The significance of this is that the modern nation state only gains its legitimacy from a practical division of functions between the centre where, as we have seen, power increasingly lies and the locality, where its subject individuals live out their everyday working and consuming lives. The original boundaries of nation-states were, of course, settled territorially. The localities they encompassed determined who were to be subjects of this rather than that nation-state. The changing of names of localities that were transferred from one to another nation-state, or when part of national territory broke free to form its own nation state, reflect the inherent dualism of states in general. The more advanced and secure states recognize this relationship constitutionally; Britain, lacking a constitution which defines the rights and duties of its citizens clearly, can have, in the absence of political consensus at the centre, a more elastic definition of the power relations between the centre and the localities.

That local differences cannot be completely effaced even by the most coercive of centralized regimes is clear from the evidence of local and regional reassertions of identity in the Soviet Union in the 1980s. Such expressions have also been part of the recent history of modern nation-states in western countries, Britain amongst them. There are signs that this defining characteristic of the modern nation-state has been recognized even in Britain's over-centralized political system. However, the discourse of local effectivity has been couched in terms of the proactivity of the private sector. Following the 1987 general election, Margaret Thatcher spoke wistfully about the Victorian city fathers who, she thought, paid from their business profits for city halls and cultural or health and educational facilities. This nostalgia incorporates a concept of individual responsibility to the locality deriving from freedom expressed in the marketplace. It is a pastiche of early modern constitutionalism based on a distorted concept of citizenship.

Locality and citizenship

As the modern nation-state cannot ignore the spatial or territorial dimension, since that is what to a large extent defines its scope and power, the locality is in fact the point at which the nation-state and its subjects interact for many of the purposes of normal life. In this respect, localities are theoretical and practical necessities in modern democracies. They are the point at which subjects with electoral rights vote, where most of the services provided by the state's welfare agencies are consumed, and where the day-to-day organization of formal and informal political resistance or proactivity towards central institutions is carried out. For example, without branches, national campaigns or institutions concerning environmental, nuclear disarmament, women's rights, trades union matters and a whole host of daily expression of citizen's rights would flounder. It is important to recognize that localities are not simply equivalent to municipalities. A great many of the freely exercised rights of combination, association, consumption, production and protest within modern society occur locally but have nothing to do with local government. Neoconservative discourse recognizes this too but wishes to squeeze much of it into either entrepreneurial activity or voluntary unpaid charity work. This position is, of course, profoundly anti-collectivist, especially anti-municipal and anti-public sector generally, in its perspective upon social and economic affairs.

Neoconservative discourse is, in the terms of this book, distinctively early modern in its perception of citizenship rights. This can easily be inferred from its regular references to 'Victorian values', 'Victorian city states' and the primacy given to the individual, the family, charitable responsibilities and so on. This is where its critique of twentieth-century modernity and that of the postmodernists part company. As we have seen, though postmodern thinking uses history, it frequently does so to point to the exclusions of later modern culture and practice. Neoconservative, early-modern revivalism seeks to add to those exclusions, especially in the sphere of citizenship rights, by redefining them more in terms of those which support a pro-market ideology. This is a crucial difference between the neoconservative project and the postmodern critique. It is worth noting in passing that neoconservatism of the Thatcherist strain has little in common with the reactionary anti-modernism of classical revivalism and community architecture. This, in turn, may help our understanding of certain of the tensions present within the British establishment between the discourse of members of the monarchy, still attached to certain of the feudal, aristocratic links between the nobility and the peasantry, and that of the New Right with its commitment to the competitive individualism of the market which dissolves such ties. The establishment of property rights was one of the first struggles to be resolved with the onset of modernity. The rights of property-owning individuals – the historical definition of the bourgeoisie – to improve the land by appropriating what had been land held in common through the Enclosure Acts, signified the rise of liberal and demise of feudal conventions, and, importantly, the exclusion from representation within the early modern state of those who owned no property, the landless poor. Such changes were the foundation of modern property law based on freedom of contract, not least because they effaced local tradition and replaced its norms with universal, abstract rules of exchange.

The contemporary reinterpretation of the early-modern concept of citizenship rights as property rights explains much of the policy package of neoconservative governments. Amongst the elements of this package are the idea of a minimalist state, a 'nightwatchman' state securing the legal and institutional rules which enable competitive exchange to function in the markets for labour, products and services. This implies the privatization of those spheres of economic life which have been absorbed by the state, such as the provision of collectively consumed services and certain of the means of production previously taken into state ownership. The individual, thus freed to be in a position to choose in a market which provides such goods and services at a competitive price, according to the economic laws of supply and demand, will become the beneficiary of a more efficient though inequitable system for distributing the social product.

This regime thus seeks, not by any means wholly successfully, to undermine the other rights which have become attached to the modern concept of citizenship. These include the equally universal categories of political, social and civil rights. The history of modernity has been that of struggles, often local in origin, to extend the definition of citizenship beyond the narrow confines of property rights. Thus the early struggles by such groups as the Chartists and their successors at the dawning of the modern era were most strongly supported in centres of working class concentration such as Lancashire, Yorkshire and South Wales. It was from such areas that the earliest representation by politicians supportive of enfranchisement and early forms of welfare came. We have seen, earlier in this book, how the formation in such regions and localities of counter cultures in the spheres of politics and welfare could act as laboratories for the future establishment of more collectivist provision of citizenship rights on a universalistic basis.

The contemporary attack by neoconservative governments on localities that, in the early 1980s, were experimenting with new, more inclusive definitions of citizenship which included sensitivity to minority demands, such as those coming from the excluded ethnic, socially deprived, sexually marginalized or gender discriminated groups, gains in significance in the light of the discussion here. Localities are often the test-beds for social innovations which seek to further citizenship rights. Similarly they can be test-beds for the implementation of New Right policies to further undermine those rights as the cases of Westminster, Wandsworth and Bradford have recently shown. The future of progressive modernity seems likely to be contested to an increasing extent on grounds of citizenship and how it is to be defined. The role of localities in acting as laboratories of social innovation seems as significant as ever, and one which may demand projecting higher up the agenda of those political parties that seek to appeal to voters with an interest in re-establishing the project of modernity upon a progressive rather than a reactionary track.

Local control and its obstacles

The vitality of this argument has already been recognized by thinkers on the Left from both eastern and western Europe who recognize that modernity in its middle and later forms, whether as the state socialism of the Soviet model or the Keynesian welfare state and Fordism of the west, has come up against certain internal contradictions.

The problems of centralized distance, insensitivity to local aspirations, the inefficiencies of bureaucratic control of welfare and the environmental degradation associated with

Figure 6 The problems of centralized distance.

untrammelled economic growth have been exposed by such writers as Rudolf Bahro and Andre Gorz. Such critiques may have helped to give rise to the remarkable internal reassessment of the assumptions of state socialism now under way under Mikhail Gorbachev's initiatives in the Soviet Union and elsewhere in the eastern bloc countries.

For the west, Gorz's ideas essentially involve an assessment of contemporary western societies as 'post-capitalist' and 'post-socialist'. This analysis is based on the perception that modern technology has created the possibility that the labour market as we have known it is being terminally undermined. Machines can produce the wealth that society distributes, workers are less necessary to the production process, the labour market as such is becoming redundant. If the labour market, which fundamentally has divided societies into class societies, can be hastened on its way out of history, then the prospects for a new classless, conflict-free society can be discerned. Central to such a society would be the provision of a general minimum income that would enable everyone to become a creative contributor to the use and distribution, hence development, of the social product and the kind of society on which that distribution is based. Local initiative would be allowed to flower within a general, democratically agreed set of planning constraints established by a responsive, sovereign state.

In a critique of this, and Bahro's more 'eco-socialist' proposals which, otherwise, share some things in common with those of Gorz, Boris Frankel has advanced the idea of 'semi-autarky', a halfway house to local self-sufficiency, as part synthesis, part alternative. He pinpoints the weakness of Gorz's argument in the belief that technology will both free workers and, somehow, cease to be controlled by the multinational corporations that are its creators as well as its owners. Take away the assumption that technology is neutrally owned and controlled, and Gorz's thesis collapses. In its place Frankel proposes a highly planned society, but also a highly democratized one. He is strongly opposed to some 'post-industrial' models of a future, more egalitarian society which advocate the replacement of nation-state power by global institutions since that, too, would play into the hands of multinational capital and the military-industrial interests. The sovereign nation-states of the modern era have to be the building blocks of the new society because to transcend market power the system has to be planned, and the maximization of democratic control requires planning to be conducted for territories of manageable proportions. Within the state system, Frankel's semi-autarkic strategy would increase democratic controls at national, regional and local levels. Most people would be employed in such state institutions and be responsible for the social wage which secured everyone's minimum income. The centre would co-ordinate the production and distribution of basic economic inputs, transport and manufactured means of production, as well as the normal taxation, military, currency, communications and diplomatic functions. Investment and trade would be centrally planned. Within this structure, local agencies would be employers, local producers and co-ordinators of the activities of their populations within the state plan.

Even though Frankel allows substantial scope for local activity and democratic influence over decisions made higher up the hierarchy, it is clear that he has not adequately understood three things about his schema. First, it remains a modernist discourse of top-down constitutional rules despite the democratic caveats he builds into his system. Second, it relies upon every other nation state in the world doing the same or comparable things. Without simultaneous world revolution that would be simply impossible. Finally, without such simultaneity, how would semi-autarkic nation states, committed to egalitarianism, be able to compete with the private, corporate organizations with whom they must continue to trade and out-perform in still existent market-based relationships? In the next chapter it will be shown just how difficult it is to escape such constraints even when localism is on the corporate agenda.

CHAPTER SIX

Post-Fordism and the flexible future

The global setting

For the foreseeable future, short of a total collapse in the
world capitalist system (which, despite certain dangerous
recent flirtations in the form of Third World credit defaults,
American indebtedness and the 1987 stock market 'meltdown'
seems unlikely), reforms in the directions suggested by the
postmodern critique and the visions of semi-autarky will
come within the framework of the institutions of modernity.
However, it is important to recognize that those institutions
are changing in significant ways in response to the various
crises of modernity itself. Some of these changes are moving
in the directions mapped out in the critique of modernity.
Amongst the most interesting are those which have already
revalued such themes as locality, difference, the combination
of discourses, recognition of 'the other', and critique of
certain inherited, monolithic norms and rules. In this book it
has been suggested that changes in economic relations
prefigure but do not necessarily determine changes in other
spheres of life. In this chapter that idea will be explored in
the context of changes visibly under way in the organization
of production. These changes are, it will be argued, quite
consistent with the more general tenor of the times which,
Margaret Thatcher notwithstanding, are decentralist, anti-
monolithic and heterogeneous.

For this to be happening the setting within which

decisions about the organization of production are made have also to have changed. One of the most important changes in setting has been the emergence in the late modern period of an increasingly integrated global economy, dominated by the most advanced forms of capitalist production and exchange. This development could be thought to run counter to the theme that has been developed thus far, namely the trend towards decentralism. Yet it is not, because the global system has no centre. It is a decentred space of flows rather than a clearly hierarchically structured space of production. There are, of course, power relations within this system, but those power relations can themselves be seen to be shifting – from, in particular, London, New York and Paris towards Tokyo – but in the process evening out somewhat, becoming more specialised and differentiated.

In Europe, despite Frankel's strictures regarding the supra-national state and economic territory, there are obvious signs that this is the way that the political economy is moving. This is already recognized in the other major trading blocs of Japan and the US, both of whom now treat the European Community as a single economic entity. Their companies are engaged in a competitive scramble to position themselves appropriately within the tariff boundaries of what could be the economic superpower of the twenty-first century. The coming of the open market in 1992 is merely the prelude to what will no doubt be a fraught debate about the growth of a European sovereignty over not only economic but political matters. Already there are diplomatic joint ventures between France and West Germany who share, experimentally, an embassy in the fastnesses of Outer Mongolia. But closer to home there is French and German co-administration of policy in the development of their border regions, and similar discussions under way between France and Spain. The emblem of a common European Community passport already exists and the debate about common citizenship of a more thoroughgoing kind has already been broached. New potential members such as Sweden, Norway, Switzerland, Austria and Turkey are having their cases for joining assessed and there has even been mention of the possibility of eastern European country membership in a future period if the Gorbachev reforms have proved they can withstand any neo-Stalinist backlash and give autonomy to the Soviet Union's satellite countries.

These, and less dramatic cross-border economic integration proposals in North and South America, point to the contemporary force of market expansion in relation to the widening and deepening powers of financial and industrial capital. Such shifts signal danger for the guardians of the modern nation-state. Margaret Thatcher's speech in 1988 at Bruges in which she ridiculed the generally supported idea of a United States of Europe is testimony to the consistency with which this strand of neoconservatism holds on to an outmoded concept of competitive national capitals set within a competitive nation-state system. The relative slowness of British industry in recognizing the challenge of the open European market, complaining about foreign takeovers while continuing and developing its traditional neo-colonial role of investing in successful corporate capital overseas, ties in with this markedly outdated view of Britain's position in relation to the rest of the world. Attitudes are changing as the deadline draws near but corporate alliances by UK firms are as much defensive as aggressive in intent towards their European partners.

Capital's response to the crisis of Fordism has been to reorganize in ways which can be surprising to those who expect normal company behaviour to be ruggedly competitive, with big fish eating little ones through takeovers and the like. For reasons that are as old as capitalism itself, namely the struggle to accumulate, large corporations throughout the developed world have of late been engaging in more co-operative behaviour than that model would suggest. Moreover, they can be seen developing co-operative links with small firms, rather than gobbling them up or closing them down. And, most strikingly of all, smaller, innovative firms have begun out-competing their larger corporate brethren. Some rather successful economic regions have owed their recent prosperity to interesting forms of economic co-operation between smaller businesses and between business and local or regional government institutions. In tune with the somewhat 'back to the futurish' theme of this book, we are seeing in some countries the revival of Marshall's idea of the industrial district. A contemporary irony could well be that as community fades in the social world, locality has been rediscovered in the economic world. This, and related 'postmodern' inversions, are discussed in what follows.

The postmodern corporation?

As was shown in Chapter 3, one of the defining characteristics of the modern corporation was its vertically integrated production organization, control being exerted from raw materials through to final product stage. Moreover, making the link between achieving mass production and the complementary mechanism of a mass marketing strategy, involving the establishment of sales networks and credit facilities, secured control of market share which was so essential to the survival of what could be a somewhat vulnerable system. This was shown on many occasions when difficulties of overproduction in a context of under-consumption posed problems for corporations, not least during the period of stagflation and the onset of 'the crisis of Fordism'. The model of organization of the Fordist corporation, hierarchized, bureaucratized, divisional, task-specified, spatially decomposed has come under attack in the contemporary management literature. What is being rejected is the 'mechanical picture' of the organization, as Michael Piore and Charles Sabel term it, in favour of something called an 'anti-organization'. The similarity between this conceptual overturning and that of Richard Rorty concerning the 'mirror of nature' approach to philosophy is striking. This is because the anti-organization is also a ferment of critical discourse in which the rules that have governed past corporate practices are there to be challenged, contradicted and placed in doubt.

Amongst the new organizational strategies of large corporations are two that are mainly directed inwardly at the internal relationship within the firm, and two outwardly directed ones aimed at rearranging relationships with other firms. The first of the internal strategies has been to use the existing divisional structure of the modern corporation but, instead of those divisions being required co-operatively to pursue the overall objectives of the corporation, they are set against each other in a system of 'internal competition'. Divisions are given greater internal autonomy to pursue their own objectives, including decisions over innovation and new product development. Such products may or may not be purchased by other divisions within the corporation depending upon their competitiveness on price and quality with the products of other companies. This strategy, pioneered by the Xerox corporation, has now been adopted by mega-corporations such as Philips and IBM.

The other main internal reorganizational restructuring within large corporations has focused upon relationships between divisions rather than within existing divisions. One of the problems with the Fordist corporate structure was its bureaucratic hierarchy and rigidity. Policy would flow downwards from the management board and if it required innovatory activity the flow might first be to the R and D division from where it would move through the testing, production engineering, operations management and marketing stages of the hierarchy so that the sales team would have the task of selling the product to a potentially recalcitrant market. The 'anti-organizational' approach has been to derigidify the organizational system, moving from a bureaucratic hierarchy to a matrix structure, again typically found in large corporations such as IBM or AT&T. This involves

144

both temporary and more long-term establishment of teams and multidisciplinary divisions in which marketing managers armed with information about the less standardized products in demand discuss the design prospects and capabilities with R and D executives and production managers. The latter managerial stratum, now of increasing importance, is thus more likely to be involved with accountants and operations managers in strategic planning deliberations because production management is the flexible pivot of the responsive corporation. Moreover, production managers, along with sales and innovation executives, are more likely to be involved in integrated product and production process discussions. What the market will bear will have implications for the length or scale of specific production runs, which in turn has implications for the kind of robotized or computerized technology likely to be required to manufacture the product to be marketed.

The two key developments in corporate external relations can be divided between those mainly with other large corporations, and those mainly with smaller firms. The change in relationships with larger corporations can be summarized under the heading of 'strategic alliance' formation. Strategic alliances are forms of pre-competitive partnership which are found in joint ventures, consortia or co-operative agreements, sometimes between firms in the same industry, such as Rover Group and Honda, or General Motors and Toyota, or increasingly between firms in different industries such as AT&T and Hewlett-Packard (telecommunications and computers) or Toshiba and VISA (electronics and credit cards). The reasons for such alliances, which have grown vastly in number during the 1980s, are threefold. First there is an increasing convergence of many technologies around the telecommunications and computers interface, with numerous sub-clusters of technologies such as electronic point of sale equipment in retailing or automatic electronic equipment in automobiles being dependent upon localized use of such technologies. Second, the costs of innovation are so high for some of these technologies that even mega-corporations prefer to collaborate on research rather than waste money in coming second in a debilitating race to the finishing line of the market place. Finally, the market for both the convergent technologies of telecommunications and computers and for either technology in its own right can be so large that only by forming alliances on a global basis can firms expect physically to be able to meet demand in the different continental submarkets. As a consequence of one or all of these imperatives large corporations are forming contracts of limited life with each other or with innovative smaller firms on, amongst other things, product R&D, process development, joint investment and joint marketing.

The second external managerial development has been with smaller innovative or even routine production companies where large corporations increasingly sub-contract production outwards from within their formerly vertically integrated system of production. Vertical disintegration, as the process is called, can arise where a smaller firm has a specialist skill which it is cheaper to buy than develop in-house, or can supply a routinely required product, component or service more cheaply than the large corporation can produce in-house. Such relationships involve the development of networking, co-operative relations, with larger corporations sometimes intervening on investment, equipment or personnel questions in the sub-contracting firms. In general, these changes imply a limited growth in the level of communication, collaboration and co-operation within and across corporate boundaries. The increased development of networking structures such as these signifies a recognition on the part of the corporate sector that difference has to be dealt with and that previously centralized decision structures have to be decentralized in more flexible, even more localized ways. Sub-contracting networks which, as will be discussed later, take an extreme form of localization in the case of the Toyota Motor Corporation in Toyota City, Japan, are setting a

146

challenge which is being emulated in localities such as Buick City, Michigan, and Fremont, California, where GM are following their ally's example.

Japanese business methods

A major stimulus to the restructuring of corporate organization along the lines discussed above has been the dramatic challenge to the hegemony of Fordist organizational systems posed by competition from Japan. If evidence were needed of the penetration of the discourse of 'the other' into mainstream western thinking, then the case of the Japanese overturning of the rational, modernist discourse of scientific management is surely the exemplar. Not only are Japanese investments eagerly sought by localities and regions in Europe and the Americas that have been stricken by deindustrialisation, but the very methods of management deployed by Japanese firms in their domestic environment are being aped with increasing regularity, albeit often in hybrid form and not without some difficulty, by western corporations.

Amongst the key organizational innovations that have been identified as contributing to the ability of Japanese companies to out-compete their western Fordist rivals on price, quality and reliability are 'just-in-time' stock-handling and 'total quality control' systems. Both innovations are social and technical and, unlike their Fordist counterparts, they incorporate the shopfloor worker into the subjective, judgemental dimension of the labour process. This contrasts with the Fordist practice of keeping the worker at a distance from such responsibilities and employing supervisors to ensure that the conceptual skill that had been extracted from labour and concentrated in the managerial structure was applied appropriately on the assembly line. Thus, rather than exaggerating the alienation of the worker from the work task the Japanese approach tends towards the absorption of her or his mental capacities into the production process.

This can be seen to some extent in the adoption of *kanban* or 'just-in-time' methods of component supply. Although originally seen as an alternative form of stock supply, it is really a method of enabling quality of products to be improved and of identifying the sources of faults in the production process. Under a Fordist mode of production organization, the corporation makes orders of parts required to produce the final product. These orders may be directed to a sub-division of the vertically integrated corporation as in the case of Ford, or more normally to an independent supplier. Traditionally the contract would stipulate price, number of components required and type. Much of the decision-making on design would be left to the supplier. The supplier's task then would be to ensure that the (normally large) batch of components was delivered to the buyer at an agreed point in the year. These components would then be stored in the stockrooms of the buyer, or sometimes for lack of space they might be stored out of doors with all the associated problems of deterioration which that implies. There was no way of controlling the quality of components, and faults would only be discovered after installation. The process was costly and inefficient. When General Motors decided to review its stock-control procedures, for example, it was discovered that savings of $9 billion could be made by moving away from this traditional method of maintaining inventories.

The just-in-time method of stock delivery places the onus upon the supplier to keep stocks at a sufficiently high level to be able to supply the buyer with components as and when needed. Michael Piore and Charles Sabel describe the system as follows:

In the *kanban* system (named for the routing slips attached to each piece in transit), suppliers are grouped closely around the final assembly plant so that the parts they supply arrive literally minutes before they are needed. In this way, the final producer is spared the costs of inventory, and defective components are spotted immediately. By contrast, in the geographically dispersed 'global sourcing' system of the world-car strategy, firms must hedge against the interruptions of supply by maintaining large inventories; these large inventories mean that a supplier may turn out batch after batch of defective parts which will not be discovered until much later, when the first bad batch is finally drawn from inventory.

By the early 1980's the advantages of the just-in-time system were so evident that American firms embraced it. They announced plans to recentralize production of many components in the Midwest, and to enter into long-term contracts with favoured suppliers. (Piore & Sabel 1984, p.201).

Thus, a relatively simple 'anti-organizational' strategy can in theory have significant effects upon the financial savings, product quality, overall efficiency and locational strategy of industries such as motor vehicles or electrical engineering where the method has been applied early.

Of course, theory and practice do not always combine perfectly. Though some American companies have modelled their supply lines on the extremely spatially concentrated model of Toyota City where the assembly plant is surrounded by numerous small and medium-sized suppliers, most, like their European counterparts are stuck with an existing, more dispersed set of supply lines. Unlike Toyota, Nissan – also a vehicle manufacturing company – does not have this concentrated urban supply and production system in Japan. Its assembly plants are located in the suburbs of larger cities and suppliers are located in other suburbs and even other cities. This pattern is reflected in Nissan's new plant in northern England where only four suppliers share its greenfield site, the majority are found in the southern half of Britain, and one-third are located in continental Europe. This means that midpoint warehouses have to be rented by suppliers or transporters, so the buyer company still saves on costs but does not maximize on timing of deliveries. Nevertheless, the quality control factor which is of key importance to Japanese industrial success is still available under this more hybrid system.

'Total quality control' is the method by which at each stage of the production process workers are expected to check for defects in parts. This process begins with the relationship between buyer and sub-contractor. Unlike the Fordist system where orders are issued but suppliers are kept at a distance, the new system involves detailed negotiations on such issues as the quality of the sub-contractor, its liquidity and so forth. Trials of sub-contractors are held amongst those who have tendered, design of the product will be specified in detail by the buyer and negotiations held regarding the costs of new equipment, labour relations and delivery capacity. The selected companies may find the buyer supplying on loan or for sale new equipment necessary to produce goods of the quality required. There is a recursive process of trial and error, sometimes lasting up to two years, before the buyer (particular if it is a Japanese buyer) is satisfied with the standards of reliability and quality of the parts for which the contract has been issued.

Once parts have arrived at the assembly line workers in the final production plant are expected to check for faults as the product moves along the line. In the Matsushita (National Panasonic) factory in South Wales, for example, the filling of printed circuit boards is part automated on machines designed by the company and part undertaken manually by women on seven parallel production lines. After each insertion of a transistor, capacitor, silicon chip assembly, speaker or whatever, the half-made television set is tested on an electronic machine, signals from which indicate whether the assembly, notably the soldering of components and wires, has been accomplished satisfactorily. Once the television tube has been inserted and the product is in its casing, testing is carried out while the set is being hit with rubber hammers to see whether or not it functions normally under stress. Even the packaging process is quality controlled for the obvious reason that a perfect product can easily be damaged in transit to the retailing outlet. In this way, Japanese products are, for comparable cost, able to outcompete most of those of their European rivals.

At both the delivery point and at the stage of final production, the components or the product are tested using statistical process control, a random approach which nevertheless covers a wide range of total possible faults. In this way, and by means of the vigilance of the employee in keeping an eye on the production of each individual product or completion of each stage in the production process, Japanese production methods have reduced faults to one part/product per million, with the aim being to get that ratio down to one part per billion in the foreseeable future.

Clearly, implementing such an exquisitely refined quality control system while keeping costs low requires a special culture of production to have been instituted. European and American companies inevitably find it hard to imitate such methods for a number of reasons. First, unlike Japanese practice, it is not normal for managers – despite in theory having taken the craft skill away from workers – actually to be able to undertake the shopfloor tasks of the production process. Managers may be accountants, computer specialists, former personnel officers or whatever, but once they become managers their contact with the shopfloor is minimal. The opposite tends to be the case in Japanese enterprises. Not only is the managing director of the company likely to have been a production engineer or manager, but all technical grades and most managerial grades of employee are expected to be able to understand the methods of production, and in a crisis to be able to take their place on the assembly line. Thus Matsushita's personnel manager sometimes sits on the assembly line when there is a staff shortage due to illness.

151

Moreover, managerial staff are always accessible to shopfloor workers whether to discuss specific problems in production or specific or general personnel matters. If a problem arises it is dealt with there and then. This managerial style is, of course, carried over into the much-vaunted single-status uniform and canteen imagery which Japanese firms display. Problematically, many western firms have taken the appearance for the reality, kitted out managers with blue overalls, closed the managerial dining room and assumed that the transformation of the company would instantly follow. Not surprisingly such superficiality does not work. Even in Japanese companies it is noticeable that employees group together according to status in the canteens, and most managers do not in fact wear the same uniform as shopfloor workers do. The advantages which Japanese companies enjoy come far more from the deep-rooted and thoroughgoing involvement of all employees in the production process.

Even such institutions as 'quality circles', which have also been adopted by many western companies seeking to emulate their Japanese competitors, tend to be disappointing where the work culture remains essentially a traditional western one. Members of quality circle teams may not be sufficiently informed or rewarded to give extra information or opinion to the company on improvements to products or production processes. A history of 'them and us', often exacerbated by the painful restructuring and regrading processes that will have preceded the introduction of 'Japanese' managerial methods in many cases, makes getting a co-operative shopfloor environment in a non-Japanese company seeking to transform its fortunes in this way difficult in the extreme. Where it has been achieved, or where a Japanese company has taken over a European one, it has sometimes meant replacing large segments of the workforce with younger or untutored operatives on the basis of 'you can't teach an old dog new tricks'.

A final element in the success of Japanese management

methods which to some extent copied the early success of Fordist methods is that generally workers in Japanese plants are well-paid. An assembly-line worker at Matsushita, for example, would expect to earn considerably more than a qualified legal secretary. Staff loyalty in what remains a basically alienating routine assembly job is thus bought by means of high wages. Moreover, in the Japanese context, as is well-known, employees receive generous welfare and other fringe benefits, although the legendary 'lifetime employment' practice has become somewhat tarnished as Japanese companies beset by the rising value of the country's currency have had to lay off workers, notably in steel and shipbuilding, with electronics and motor vehicles beginning to follow suit, and seek inward investment opportunities in other countries. Outside Japan the fringe benefits are not so generous, partly because of the existence of welfare states in the host economies. Nor are they so generous in less developed countries in South-East Asia to which Japanese firms have been migrating to seek out cheap labour and where welfare states do not exist.

At the end of the day, Japanese success is built on creating a culture of incorporation within the workplace, as a result of which employers extract more effort from their own employees than is the case with western companies. Added to that is the widespread practice of sub-contracting work out to smaller companies that are usually too small to be unionized. Accordingly the parts that are purchased are both cheaper and of higher quality than the equivalents produced under a Fordist system. Though Japanese companies are content to have unionized workers in their western plants, they insist on single-union representation and often 'no-strike' clauses in their union agreements. The Japanese approach, which heralds a post-Fordist era of production organization, is based on a more intensive form of exploitation of labour and therein lies its success over its more extensive Fordist predecessor.

Post-Fordist technology and labour

Amongst the more important changes in factory organization, some of which apply also to the reorganization of office work, have been those concerning the type of technology used and the organization of labour within the overall production process. The key term linking together these different aspects of the modern factory or office regime is *flexibility*. We have seen already how managerial organization has been moving, in some leading cases, away from a bureaucratic, hierarchical structure towards a more flexible set of relationships between hitherto separate divisional executives. Moreover, Japanese management and production methods involve improving the degree of flexible response companies can make to the problem of defective components. Added to this is the personal and collective flexibility of management to shopfloor requirements. However, flexibility is far more pervasive than this in the post-Fordist firm, and although relatively few totally flexible firms yet exist many have moved some way towards implementing flexible production methods in pursuit of the ideal.

Flexibility is increasingly built into the technology used in contemporary workplaces. Word processors, personal computers, work stations and numerous other technological aids are common in the office nowadays. In the factory, computerized technologies have invaded significant areas of the production process. Amongst the first of these have been computer aided design (CAD) and computer numerically controlled machine tools (CNC). In the Fordist design office there would, typically, have been an army of draughtsmen and draughtswomen working on the engineering blueprints that were the basic output from the design office and input into the production process. Such designs were detailed, costly and rigid. The production process demanded this since it was itself relatively rigid, with process machinery dedicated to the repetitive production of identical parts to fit into standardized products.

Figure 7 Fordism and Post-Fordism: the changing face of production.

Mass production under Fordism was volume production for a mass market with only relatively superficial changes being made from model to model or year to year. As markets changed and consumers began to demand less standardized products so the production process had to be changed to speed up the variations that could be played on a single theme. More recently a stage has been reached, known as programmable assembly, where a range of different items can be produced on the same assembly line. CAD is a first step in enabling that process to occur.

Computerized design systems enable mock-ups of products to be produced on the computer rather than on blueprints which are then transformed into lifesize models of the prototype. They require a data base of information on the multitude of componentry to be incorporated in the product as well as a library of different design solutions to the problem posed by managerial interpretation of what the market requires. Often the CAD system will be the centrepiece of a work station which attracts a cluster of designers, engineers and draughtspersons around it, each feeding in different elements of the overall design process. Variations in design within the parameters of the different market segments at which the product(s) are aimed can be experimented with far more rapidly and conclusively than in the traditional design office. CAD provides opportunities for draughting skills to be deployed more creatively in theory, but traditional draughtspersons can be displaced in large numbers by the introduction of such systems, so in general only a few benefit from the technological innovation.

CNC and programmable machine tools enable production to be changed from one product to another by means of a change in the instructions provided to the assembly machinery and the automatic lathes that produce the complicated parts comprising engines, gearboxes and so on in, for example, the motor vehicle industry. This means that instead of producing a long line of identical products, a company can produce batches of a mixture of product types without the disadvantage of having the line shut down while retooling takes place. Programmable machinery and assembly thus enables considerable cost savings to be made by comparison with traditional Fordist technology. Flexible response to variations in market demand is therefore possible. These technologies can be used in small firms as well as large mass production factories and they signify the emergence of what economists call 'economies of scope' to complement and in some cases challenge the more typical 'economies of scale' which Fordist industry first exploited to the fullest extent.

The next stage of development, reached so far by relatively few firms, is to link together CAD and CNC technology to produce a computer aided manufacturing or even a computer integrated manufacturing system which would incorporate robotized assembly techniques for certain parts of the production process. At its fullest extent an assembly line organized in this way would be a full-blooded flexible manufacturing system, probably incorporating just-in-time delivery systems, and total quality control using automated statistical process control. In such a system, which is on the way, but very expensive and obviously prone to problems of adjustment and breakdown, the place of the shopfloor worker is threatened with virtual extinction, as, for example, has happened in modern steelworks.

This raises the question of the role of labour in the post-Fordist flexible production system. There are four dimensions to the changes being experienced by workers, especially shopfloor workers, under contemporary economic conditions. Underpinning these four dimensions are two important characteristics of modern society generally, and the labour market in particular, as the mechanism which is mainly responsible for the changing distribution of income. As was shown in Chapter 5, British society is polarizing in social class terms. A similar change can be observed in US society and, to a less pronounced degree, in other advanced societies also. This polarization is a product, in part, of

157

technological changes in the workplace, changes in government policy, and the effects of overseas competition.

Technological change of the kind that has been described has particularly negative effects upon the workforce in many industries. As we have seen in the case of draughtspersons confronted with the introduction of CAD, the new technology displaces human labour – one estimate is that the introduction of CAD can reduce the draughting labour demand by at least a half in an average-sized company. Similarly, the introduction of robots to undertake tasks previously done by people has obvious labour-displacing effects. And the application of programmable assembly means that there is less demand for the skilled craftsmen who used to be responsible for retooling the transfer machinery in the typical Fordist production plant. In many and various ways new technology reduces the demand for operators and certain traditionally skilled grades of workers.

Government policies have further assisted this process, in Britain at least, in two main ways. First, by pursuing monetarist policies to cure inflation, interest rates were raised to a level where companies found it difficult both to borrow investment capital and to export output because of the overvaluation of the currency. As a consequence many companies went bankrupt as the government pursued such policies with the justification that they were making companies 'leaner but fitter'. In reality such policies were destroying the industrial base, a factor which was apparent at the time of their fiercest implementation in 1981–2. This has now been made reapparent by the failure of British industry to meet expanding demand in the economy because of the limited capacity that has remained as a source of domestic supply. The surge of imports consequent on the manufacturing consumer boom of the late 1980s has threatened the British economy with disastrous spiralling inflation as a consequence. Meanwhile many of the workers who could have been put to work to meet that demand remain idle.

The second government policy that has contributed to labour displacement has been the legislative attack upon trades union law. The limitations upon trades unions to defend the rights and interests of their members have encouraged employers to disregard union responses to large-scale redundancy programmes, implemented as a first-stage response to the problems of liquidity posed by government monetary policy and the effects of foreign competition. The largest proportion of workers to have been made redundant have been those in the lowest, operator grades, as a study of the British engineering industry carried out in the mid-1980s showed. All grades of employee except scientists, technologists and professional engineers had fallen between 1978 and 1984. But whereas draughtspersons had experienced a 20 per cent decline and craftsmen 30 per cent, operators and other low-graded occupations had declined by 42 per cent.

Foreign competition has been the cause of both the preceding changes for without the surge of cheaper, high quality products entering the British market since the 1970s, restructuring could have been managed much more humanely. Nevertheless, the loss of markets at home and overseas meant that, once again, the argument for saving costs, thereby perhaps saving the firm, by means of workforce rationalization was unassailable. One response of many firms was to export domestic production to cheap labour zones in Third World countries, thereby adding to the import of unemployment signified by the increased levels of imports of products from overseas-based companies. The export of British investment capital to those same, successful overseas producer countries further exacerbated the prospects for growth in domestic industry.

But technological change, and to some extent government policies, have also contributed to the opposite pole of the bifurcating class structure. For the demand for highly qualified technologists, scientists and other professionals in industry, both manufacturing and service based, has grown

159

very rapidly as the installation of automated machinery has expanded in post-Fordist conditions. Government taxation changes have helped make such relatively highly paid occupations even more remunerative, but even so demand continues to outstrip supply in what remains a tight labour market. Government training policies tended to result in greater attention being devoted to the requirement that schools, polytechnics and universities expand the provision of training and qualifications for such occupational groups, while focusing less attention initially upon the technological re-equipping of redundant operator-grade workers. As a general consequence of the concentration of these three tendencies income polarization has developed to a considerable extent in the past decade.

Taking advantage of these needs and opportunities in the labour market companies have been able to move towards the development of flexible workforces. The first kind of change worth considering is the development of what has been called *functional flexibility*. This applies to both professional or qualification-grade workers and shopfloor workers, but for the moment the focus will be upon the former. The advent of computers has created a demand for multi-skilled technical workers capable of adjusting and adapting the software embodied in such machinery. But, more importantly, the fragility of the systems has enhanced the role of the personnel required to maintain them. Such workers may have to exercise managerial, engineering and technical skills as well as those crossing boundaries between mechanical engineering, electronics engineering and software programming. Where once they were more specialised, now they are jacks-of-all trades. Other functionally flexible developments can be found in offices where word processors now enable secretaries in insurance and legal firms to undertake tasks, such as routine underwriting and contract preparation, that were previously the province of lower managers.

A second kind of flexibility increasingly to be found in the labour market is the phenomenon of *numerical flexibility*. This applies more to shopfloor than managerial workers, although it applies increasingly to specialist technologists whose skills may be required only for a relatively short term during a period of installation of new technologies. Such expertise as that associated with software programming or systems engineering would fall into the numerically flexible category; some such workers might be self-employed, more are likely to be permanently employed in specialist consultancies. The underlying feature of both upper- and lower-grade numerically flexible workers is that they are employed on short-term contracts. They are brought in and let go from employment according to the particular demands of the company in question. In the idealized model of the 'flexible firm' such workers may be self-employed so that when orders fall off the company can release them without having to make redundancy payments. Although there has been a history of the use of numerically flexible workers in industries that are seasonal by nature, the reasons for requiring numerical flexibility nowadays are more likely to be related to short-term non-seasonal market fluctuations. The availability of pools of redundant workers familiar with procedures in their former full-time employment makes the targeting of numerically flexible workers at the lower occupational levels relatively straightforward. Companies such as the British Steel Corporation, Nissan and some high technology companies are examples of those making frequent use of numerical flexibility.

A further form of flexibility in the workforce which also enables employers to cut the costs of labour directly and indirectly – by not having to pay redundancy and other disbursements – is part-time working. There has been a general growth in the proportion of part-time working in the advanced countries during the 1970s and 1980s. The highest rate of increase displayed has been in the Netherlands where the rate rose from 4 per cent to 50 per cent between 1973 and 1981 while in southern European countries such as

Greece and Italy it remains at less than 10 per cent. The reason for that is probably because of unregistered part-time work in the informal sector or 'black economy'. Wherever part-time working is found it is overwhelmingly a female activity. Rates of female involvement in part-time working range from 63 per cent in Greece to 94 per cent in Britain. Though many of these part-time women workers are involved in manufacturing industry, the overwhelming majority are employed in services, such as cleaning, catering, shop assistants and so on.

Finally, given these different varieties of flexible occupation, what is implied for the nature of work in the post-Fordist factory or office? The term that deals with this dimension is 'flexible working practices'. The general aim of companies has been to reduce demarcation lines between workers' activities in the workplace. Under Fordism and scientific management it will be recalled that work was divided in detail by task specification. Trades unions soon recognized that demarcation was an important element in industrial relations since it enabled them to protect members' jobs and to bargain for increased remuneration when job tasks were changed, as, for example, when new technology was introduced. However, from industry's viewpoint, this led to 'overmanning' and, during the period of Fordist crisis, gave a justification for making labour redundant, especially as trades unions were in a generally weaker negotiating position at such a time than hitherto. Thus there have been major regradings of workers' occupational and job specification criteria to introduce practices whereby a mechanical engineer will do certain electrical engineering tasks, or a machine operator will be expected to perform relatively simple maintenance tasks involving either skill, instead of waiting by a defective machine until the technical expertise of the maintenance worker can be brought in to fix it. As we have seen, under Japanese working conditions managers can be expected to be able to fill in for machine operators at short notice, though this is unusual.

Thus both technological and labour force change have been loosening up the more rigid structures inherited from the Fordist era. The belief on the part of management in many industries is that flexibility is more efficient, more productive and generally cheaper. However, the fact that such combinations of flexibility may now be generally required in the different kinds of plant that a multi-locational company may operate has certain implications for the geographical structure of the corporation. Whereas under Fordism the functional and spatial division of labour between managerial, research, marketing, craft engineering, and assembly work meant that routine activities could be decentralized to localities where no special skills were required of the workforce except those coming from brief, on-the-job training, post-Fordism has other requirements.

Whether in respect of the growing dependence of buyer firms on their specialist sub-contractors, the emergent matrix structures of management which bring together divisional representatives for regular discussions, or the demands for a combination of highly skilled functionally flexible workers and casually hired numerically flexible workers, the prospects for decentralizing branch plants to locations where ordinary semi-skilled workers are abundant seem to be diminishing. There may not be a complete reconcentration of activity back to a tightly knit locality such as Toyota City, as implied by the just-in-time model, but it is likely that only large cities or urban agglomerations can satisfy such diverse networking requirements. The exception would be where new investments are made on greenfield locations and a new work culture is itself 'manufactured' on site.

Industrial localities

Japanese business methods signify a revival of an early modern, neo-paternalist method of incorporating the worker into something approaching an industrial 'community' with its own distinctive character. Other features of post-Fordist flexibility also go, to some extent, 'back to the future' for inspiration. The casualization of labour working on temporary contracts is a case in point, as is the revival of sub-contracting, thought only a decade ago to be an anachronistic survival from pre-Fordist days; and the move towards matrix structures of management points to a recognition of the importance of communication across hitherto sacrosanct boundaries within the corporation, as do the networks of strategic alliances outside it.

Many of these motifs combine in what is perhaps the most remarkable development of the post-Fordist era, the revival of the eighteenth- and nineteenth-century phenomenon of the *industrial district*. Nineteenth-century industrial districts, as described by Alfred Marshall, were systems of small, craft-based companies specialized in the production of a particular set of products, interlinked by tight networks of sub-contractors, often organized around family relationships, dependent on starting finance raised within the community and capable of producing customized products, often for a luxury market. Such districts would be localized in particular regions or even within towns or specialized areas of cities. The best examples of industrial districts were the Sheffield cutlery, tools and special steels district, the Birmingham armaments and jewellery quarters, the Lyons silk manufacturing district, the New York garment district and the Roubaix and Kortrijk textile towns of France and Belgium.

In recent years it has become apparent that such localities not only survive in the contemporary period but they are amongst the most dynamic, fast-growing centres of production in the 'postmodern' space economy. Nowadays industrial localities tend not to be found so commonly in their classic nineteenth-century locations because of capital concentration and the move towards satisfying mass market demand by Fordist production methods, though this is by no means universally true. The new industrial localities are more frequently to be found in southern Europe, though their discovery there has led to the search for them elsewhere, and it seems that new ones are also to be found in parts of northern Europe and even North America.

The most prominent contemporary industrial localities are those of north-central Italy where the phenomenon first drew attention. Similar though less developed versions exist in the Aveiro region of Portugal which specializes in metal goods, the Barcelona and Basque regions of Spain where there are specialisms in cotton and woollen textiles and machine-tool manufacture respectively, and, to a limited extent, in Greece near Missalongi on the Gulf of Corinth and the northern provinces of Macedonia and Thrace where textiles and leather-working specialisms are concentrated. In northern Europe, the Jutland region of Denmark has become an important centre of small-scale, luxury clothing production relatively recently, while in West Germany the Baden-Württemburg region has numerous such localities specialized in the production of textiles, machine tools and motor vehicle components.

In the contemporary context the small firms comprising these industrial localities tend to be characterized more pronouncedly in the northern European and Italian cases by their use of the most advanced computerized technology from automated laser cutting machines to the use of programmable assembly for the production of small batches of manufactured goods, often designed to order. In the Italian case, as we shall see, these specialisms have progressed merely from the use to the manufacture of such computerized technologies and diversification of skills into the software and specialist systems engineering expertise associated with such innovations. Probably the most advanced new industrial localities from which such micro-electronic products and expertise originated are the high technology complexes of Silicon Valley and Orange County in California and the Route 128 axis around Boston, Massachussetts.

The Italian industrial localities are found in a swathe from

Veneto in the north-east to Marche on the borders of the Mezzogiorno. Knitted goods are concentrated in Treviso and Carpi, textiles in Como and Prato, special machines in Parma and Bologna, hydraulic devices in Modena, ceramic tiles in Sassuolo, agricultural implements in Reggio Emilia, and shoes, tableware and musical instruments in Ancona. Some of these localities are old and well-established, some have emerged quite recently, the level of technology used can vary within and between them, and the markets they supply can be local, but more normally are national, even international. They often correspond with the areas where, historically, the 'putting-out' system operated. This, of course, was a characteristic form of industrial organization preceding the onset of the modern era where an entre-preneur provided raw materials to family businesses and then supplied the finished product to the market. In areas where expertise in small-scale business management was retained despite the advance of modern, Fordist industrial methods, the traditional system could be adjusted to the demands of the more segmented markets of the late modern period.

In simplified terms, and if for convenience we ignore the widespread existence of the traditional artisan, found everywhere in Italy, there seem to be two main models whereby industrial localities emerge. The first is where dependent sub-contractors change from serving principally a local market to becoming part of a large corporation's vertical disintegration plans. This type of development was typical of the first stage of growth in the engineering localities of Emilia-Romagna, the region centred upon Bologna. This model later developed into the second model, where a system of sub-contracting small firms link into a network specialized in a specific industry and their market is immediately national, then international. This is more typical of developments in the Veneto region where different clothing sub-markets exist for each stage of the production process – weaving, finishing, cutting, stitching of garments, for example.

There may also be relevant political differences in the regional culture which hasten the progress from one to another or within a particular model. Veneto, for example, is a Catholic, conservative or 'white' region. The attitude of local and regional government is non-interventionary, enabling entrepreneurs to develop as and where they please and with relatively little concern for environmental controls or wages and conditions of workers. It is in this context that the most celebrated small-firm 'multinational', Benetton, based in Treviso, has grown. It is a family-owned firm which produces only designs; every other aspect of production is sub-contracted locally, nationally and even internationally. Its sub-contractors often use the most advanced textile production machinery and the company franchises its retail outlets, now found in most countries of the world. The company is thus a highly integrated network with marketing data being relayed back from the shops to headquarters on a daily basis.

By contrast, the engineering industries in Emilia Romagna, a Communist, or 'red', region began to take off in the 1960s and 1970s when large Fordist industries, notably Fiat, experienced severe labour relations difficulties and sought to disintegrate the production of parts vertically to dependent sub-contractors to keep costs down. They found the local agricultural machinery companies of Bologna, Modena and Parma ideal for their purposes. However, such companies tended, as with most small firms, to operate an over-exploitative form of labour relations, with low wages and poor conditions. The local and regional governments began to intervene to improve conditions but in exchange offered financial aids and a range of services such as assistance in co-operative developments, provision of industrial parks and infrastructure, employer advice on marketing, technology and accountancy, workforce training and software development. In addition, land use development and pollution have been controlled such that quality of life is relatively unaffected by the development process.

The development of industrial localities containing firms using and advancing the sophisticated machinery more normally associated with large corporations, accruing economies of 'scope' through flexible specialization and integration, which when successfully exploited can turn into economies of 'scale', as in the case of Benetton or its smaller rival, Stefanel, points to the remarkable innovative capacity of the post-Fordist organization of production. For not only are such industrial localities able to out-compete their more Fordist neighbours, they are causing them to copy these more flexible arrangements. Capital concentration is, however, occurring as large firms acquire some of the more successful small firms. But the interventionary role of local and regional government in aiding and controlling the negative aspects of industrialisation is suggestive of a possible future development of localities as relatively autonomous defenders of their own identity, and even the revival of a contemporary, proactive concept of community.

CHAPTER SEVEN

Conclusions. Modernity and locality: critique and renewal

It is ironic that as this book has traced the demise of everyday relationships centred on the family, kinship, co-operation and custom (the classic definition of *community*) something akin to community seems to be re-emerging in the workplace. As market relations, and in some contexts the definition of citizenship as freedom to consume based on economic choice, penetrate ever deeper into our perceptions of what it is to be a normal, modern individual, communal relations seem to be pervading business. It is, of course, possible to draw this contrast beyond stretching point. Production remains fundamentally aimed at opening up and expanding those very market relations which have every-where undermined community. The overriding reason for the rediscovery of communality is the failure of the ideology of modern centralism, bureaucracy and hierarchy with their 'Weberian' rules regarding the definition and organization of knowledge. Meanwhile, the critique of modernity has given rise to theories about aesthetics, jurisprudence, philosophy and society, and to practice in local politics and business, which put importance on the idea of *locality*.

The critique of modernity from those in philosophy, fiction, architecture and the law who have been labelled postmodernists remains a critique. It offers no obvious alternative project to that of modernity. On the contrary, the value of that critique has been in precisely identifying the repressive elements that have inscribed the practical

169

development of the various institutions of modernity.

It can appear on superficial acquaintance with certain of the diverse strands of critique that all share the same pervasive discontent with modernity and its works and wish to see it overthrown completely. But on closer inspection it is relatively easy to identify the two in particular which fundamentally part company with the general themes adopted by the postmodernists. One is reactionary anti-modernism which appeals nostalgically to a pre-modern 'golden age', when aristocratic values ruled the aesthetic sphere and *noblesse oblige* involved a recognition of the duties of privilege towards the dependent masses. This kind of critique or rejection can, by definition, have little other than a superficial appeal to those uneasy about, but with inadequately formulated responses to, their discontent, particularly with the visual appearance of modernity. There seems little demand for a return to the absolutism which reactionary anti-modernism implies.

The other, more powerful, strand of critique is that associated with the neoconservative politics of the Right. Latching on to those generalized discontents with the monolithic forms of modernity represented by Keynesianism, the welfare state, even Fordist monopolization, the neo-conservative project is not anti-modernist but seeks to efface the achievements of mature modernity by returning to the basic principles of its earliest phase. Of crucial importance to this version of modernity is a concept of the citizen emancipated by freedom of contract and property law subject principally to the workings of the 'invisible hand' of the market and a recognition of the supreme sovereignty of the state as defender of the moral and social order.

The history of modernity has shown that this narrow definition of citizenship was rapidly perceived to be inadequate in meeting the needs of individuals freed to engage in unequal exchange. The quest for equality was the motive force for the gradual redefinition of citizenship to include political, social, welfare and civil rights and the development of those institutions which now appear as blockages to future growth. In practice it is not the content, but the form of the institutions of mature modernity that began to earn criticism not only from the radical Right but the political Left also. Questions regarding the definition of citizenship in narrow neo-market terms are rising up the political agenda as the limitations upon freedom in non-market spheres are beginning to be questioned. History may not repeat itself, power relations and political struggles ensure the relative indeterminacy of outcomes, but this particular historic struggle, over the extension of rights to democratic representation, collectively provided welfare services, and consideration for excluded minorities shows signs of re-forming as the contradictions of New Right reductionism begin to unfold in the Catch 22 of, for example, inflationary prescriptions which further exacerbate inflationary problems.

Control of the state apparatus was always, and correctly, perceived by progressive reform parties as the only way to curb the creative destruction imposed on society by the unleashing of modern capitalism. But the power that the reforms of the maturer phases of modernity embodied in Keynesianism and welfarism sought to control has itself moved on beyond the level of the modern nation state. We are now clearly in a stage of economic integration that is continental before it is national and increasingly global before it is either. In this context the policy instruments of the modern nation-state ought logically to be pointed increasingly outwards beyond national boundaries rather than inwards and downwards at limiting hard-won citizenship rights (other than those of 'freedom in the marketplace'). This is why the utopia of semi-autarky is no solution to the problems of modernity. Modernity has already moved on; we have a global and continental market system and in Europe, embryonic supranational state institutions in the making. Without resorting to slogans such as 'think global, act local', the thought might nevertheless occur that the time

171

has come to reverse the order to 'think local, act global'. In other words strong, inwardly directed, centralist controls, such as those exerted under neoconservative hegemony in Britain already appear anachronistic by comparison with developments in diverse fields in the rest of the world.

The unexplored question is how might such a response, informed by the critique of modernity, take practical form in a 'postmodern' world which would, in fact, be a continuation of the project of modernity by other means? Several of the elements can, on the basis of the analysis of contemporary changes already proposed, be identified, at least in outline. To begin where the postmodern critique of the rigidities of modernity seems, in many ways, to have proceeded furthest in terms of practical action – at the factory gates – it is clear that the two most interesting developments have been in the global and local dimensions in recent years. In the process, the powers of many of the medium-sized nation-states, and even of some of the largest, are now increasingly circum-scribed by developments in the international economy. Even the capacity of the largest multinational corporations to manage markets seems to be being challenged by the emergence of potential 'super-markets', not only in Europe but, not unimaginably, in the Soviet bloc and the largest underdeveloped markets such as those, further down the road, in China, India and Latin America. The formation of new kinds of collaboration and co-operation by giants such as General Motors and Toyota, Ford and Nissan, Philips and Sony, Siemens and GEC signify the realization that stand-alone competition is no longer a serious option in the frantic race to maintain market position and develop market opportunities. The acceptance of the importance of markets and international technology transfer as key sources of both economic and social innovation in the Communist countries seems likely to provide the boost that capitalist production required to break out of the vicious stagflationary circle that assailed it during the crisis of Fordism. It is perhaps also to these countries that modernity will have to migrate, as it were, to receive its new injections of energy in the creative, aesthetic sphere, as it has, in limited ways, through its reception and interpretation in parts of the developing world.

But it is also at the level of the locality that the practices of post-Fordist industry seem likely to have a major impact. Despite the centrifugal tendencies implied by the growth of an apparently untethered global space of economic flows, in practice economic activity touches base in key locations, but also receives its internal challenges to restructure from socio-economic innovations that can be geographically highly specific, as we have seen. For the growth of markets also involves their increasing segmentation, a factor which means that although mass production remains an imperative of the economic system, standardization and its technological substructure has become less of a necessity. The quest to satisfy markets that, in the west, seem to be becoming increasingly aestheticized by designer labels and customized or application-specific requirements, implies a continuation of the pursuit of economies of scope at the lowest feasible cost if the advantages of economies of scale are to be reappropriated.

In this search for low-cost efficiency and innovation there is a revaluation of the role of the localized complex, whether of sub-contracting small firms feeding parts into production 'just-in-time' to meet corporate requirements, or of industrial localities acting both co-operatively and competively to fill the niche markets of designer demand. Those localities that are proactively positioned to anticipate or respond to the new needs of intermediate or final demand will be the ones to reap advantage from the changing mode of production. But this implies a throat-cutting 'zero-sum' game between localities acting for themselves in beggar-thy-neighbour fashion towards each other. This is not the only option, however; there is also the positive-sum game of inter-locality specialization with collaboration on questions of information sharing and joint action in respect of provision of specialist services. Left alone, market devices usually do produce zero-sum outcomes in which one locality's gains are another one's losses. So there is a role for state or supra-state regulation to minimize negative outcomes. But such regulation might, in some instances, be far more appropriate being organized from the bottom-up rather than in centralist top-down fashion. The bottom can never adequately deal with questions of currency exchange rates or other macro-economic matters but the knitting together of local resources within more micro-economic firm-level and inter-firm relations might more appropriately be left to local initiative.

It is perhaps instructive that one aspect of the success of Italian industrial localities has arisen from the close affiliation between local artisans and entrepreneurs or co-operative members, and local political parties whether of left or right persuasion. In Britain, for example, while it has been a normal expectation that Conservatively controlled local administrations will act in such a way as not to hinder entrepreneurial activity unwarrantedly, this has usually been realized in forms of municipal conservatism associated with 'keeping down the rates' and penny-pinching attitudes to local expenditure. Labour and other left-of-centre parties have usually been closely associated with sympathies and policies favourable towards the consumption needs of their less affluent residents (housing, social services, etc.) but have seldom had the close understanding, even affiliation, of the sort of artisanate that forms an important element of local and regional political support for the Communist parties of Tuscany or Emilia Romagna. In localities in those regions the informal transmission of information within the local body politic is a key factor in the success of local economic strategy and enterprise. There are cross-local complementarities in operation in such a system which could profitably be emulated elsewhere.

This consideration leads conveniently on to the question of local policy-making and the scope and constraints of localities within and beyond the remit of local government.

In many western countries, including Britain, there has been a notable growth of interest and activity in the prospects of encouraging local economic development of the kind we have seen operating in the Italian industrial localities. In some instances, notably in Michigan, officers of the governor's cabinet council have implemented policies modelled on Italian flexible integration for those motor vehicle components suppliers left high and dry by the crisis of Fordism in and around Detroit, and excluded from the privilege of being engaged in the recently established just-in-time subcontracting networks. In London under the Greater London Council industrial strategy, completed shortly before the abolition of the council, a similar model was being proposed to link together smaller and medium-sized, often family-owned firms, with attention being paid especially to quality of work considerations. Latterly other localities such as Newcastle-upon-Tyne have sought to follow suit with the idea of helping facilitate local 'synergy' in the small-firm and sub-contracting sectors of the local economy.

It has frequently been argued that the relative paucity of equivalent signs of local economic growth to those displayed elsewhere are a problem caused by lack of local finance either as an investment fund for firms or as a resource for the local authority to invest in economic and physical services and infrastructure. However, the real problem is one of time. The new Italian industrial localities have often taken twenty or thirty years to mature, the older ones may even be dated back to the middle ages.

In some of the recent analyses of the success of Italian industrial localities, the following important evaluative points have been made. First, in most cases the local availability of capital or savings seems to have been an irrelevance to the emergence of small businesses or co-operatives. The capital invested was primarily human in a context where working was often traded off against leisure. Northern European attitudes, acculturated by Fordist norms

175

of working time and leisure time, might find this apparent inversion of the stereotype of southern European relaxedness somewhat hard to take, but there it is. However, it is one thing to work hard in ignorance and unproductively, and another to work in a context where there is knowledge that can usefully be applied to the achievement of objectives. There is normally both an informal and a formal system of expertise in such localities. The traditional business knowledge derived from the putting-out system is supplemented and increasingly transcended by the existence and widespread acquisition of knowledge from a network of technical education schools providing business skills. This is something clearly within the scope of local training agencies to supply, and it is likely to be of equal or greater importance to the fortunes of the local economy than the provision of other more practical day-to-day services, important as those such as marketing, accountancy and especially retraining must undoubtedly be.

Nevertheless, the question of local sources of finance cannot simply be swept away by the espousal of puritanical work norms. Even within an increasingly centralized control of the budgetary autonomy of localities there remain sources of finance that are untapped in many European contexts. The American practice of enabling municipalities to establish quasi-independent public development authorities which raise finance by issuing bonds secured against the return from revenue charged for the use of the facility in which capital is invested might be one such innovation which even a Thatcher government would, it might be thought, welcome as a market transaction. However, even that possible opportunity looks likely to be closed off by recommendations contained in local government finance legislation. The innovative enterprise boards which some more adventurous, often radically leftwing municipalities established in the larger metropolitan county councils, many of which have survived the abolition of their democratically elected parents, would be an ideal vehicle for pursuing such a strategy. But for the moment, as we have seen, less radical organizations such as Lancashire Enterprises Ltd must have recourse to the international banking fraternity to raise the relatively modest sums they need to assist the reindustrialization of one or two localities.

A post-Thatcher administration might have cause to relax many of the controls on local public sector resources and expenditure. However, the temptation to retain the relatively undemocratic centralized structures set in place in the Thatcher regime may prove too inviting to resist as a mode of local service delivery based on centrally determined norms. Such seems to be the danger implicit in thinking in the political centre rather than on the Left, where such instruments as the urban development corporations are perceived as far more efficient deliverers of urban redevelopment policies than their more democratic local government predecessors. There even seems to be some enthusiasm for the withering away of the traditional local authority and its replacement by unelected regional and local development authorities modelled on the urban development corporations. This is the continuation and development of centralism by other means. For while it is indisputable that urban development corporations have delivered results with some efficiency in the booming Docklands area of London, they have been less impressive elsewhere. Moreover, it is now clear that they have generally socially regressive effects in squeezing out poorer citizens from cheaper inner city locations by providing the urban spectacle and hyperreality of warehouse conversions, high technology parks and architectural extravaganzas which appeal particularly to the younger, affluent, gentrifying strata of contemporary society.

The question of socially regressive policy instruments leads into a consideration less of the job-creating prospects of local initiative than the continuation of capacity to provide or even increase the services of a local welfare state. Under the centralism of neoconservative strategy the responsibilities of local councils to provide basic services in housing and

177

Figure 8 Doubtful benefits of inner city development.

education have been undermined by recent legislation. Council tenants now have the right to elect an alternative landlord to the local authority if they are dissatisfied with its performance. Similarly, parents have the right to remove control of local schools from local authorities if they can muster a majority in favour of having it funded directly by the Department of Education. Here the critique of certain aspects of municipal management from the Left of the political spectrum meet up with the critique from the Right to produce not a decentralist but an even more centralist or, in the case of housing, a private market solution, which will inevitably add to the social segregration and class polarization of contemporary society.

Yet ideas of tenants' control of council housing estates have had a lengthy provenance in more radical Left circles where the insensitivity and inefficiency of even local bureaucracies became causes for criticism. In some Labour-controlled local authorities tenants' management committees have quite successfully taken over the day-to-day responsibilities of running housing estates. This strand of thinking echoes a tradition of popular control of certain kinds of welfare service that was lost with the onset of late modernity and the installation of a universalist welfare state. Local health, welfare and leisure – and even adult education – services have a history of having been successfully managed from within working-class communities outside the purview of either the local or the central state. An incoming leftist or even centre-leftist government could at some point wish to take account of local capacity to manage important social affairs in proposing improvements both to the centralism of the Old Left and that of the New Right.

These are by no means 'post-industrial utopias' that have been outlined. Many of their foundations are already in place. The postmodern critique of modernity points in one very clear direction, towards a decentralist continuation of the project of modernity. It is worth noting, in passing, that even the architecture which, rebelliously, became endowed with the label 'postmodern' has recently been relabelled 'modern classicism' as though the prospect of losing textual touch with the wellsprings of emancipation that came with the rise of modernity was too painful to contemplate. The perception may be growing that modernity needs not to be overwhelmed but rather to be thoroughly overhauled to restore its essentially viable but somewhat timeworn principles.

This book has sought to show that there is considerable validity to the critique of modernity but that the critique, from whichever angle it is directed, leaves the main edifice intact. Against more apocalyptic observers of the contemporary scene who perceive in the ever deeper market penetration of modern consciousness the increasing power of the mass media to fill our minds with often meaningless sign systems, and the growing individuation and privatism of home-centred entertainments of various kinds, a death or dissolution of social ties, the argument has been made that such ties may now be being remade in new ways. The homogeneity of mass society formed in some measure by the organizational structures of Keynesianism, welfarism and Fordism is giving way to a more differentiated, pluralistic set of discourses and social relations.

Amongst the more significant of these are the emergent trend towards a revival of localism, with particular pertinence in some of the co-operative tendencies found in post-Fordist business organization, the initiatives being taken in many localities to try to create employment opportunities, and the as yet prefigurative possibilities regarding the revival of pre-Fordist methods of delivering local welfare services. Moreover, in the cultural sphere there are signs of a growing interest in recovering, albeit in styles which are often more hyperrealistic than realistic, local identity in the form of local museums, local architectural vernaculars and festivals in the arts, music and literature. To some extent these shifts are constrained, even blocked, by an anachronistic centralism which has sought to distort and reduce citizenship to an early modern concept of freedom to choose in the market place. This is ultimately inconsistent with the democratic impulses inherent both in the project and the critique of modernity. Localism may yet be a key agent in dissolving such blockages and distortions, thus propelling modernity onto a higher plane than has yet been imagined.

References

The main texts referred to in this book are as follows:

Auster, P. 1988. *City of Glass*. In *The New York trilogy*. London, Faber.

Bahro, R. 1984. *From red to green*. London: Verso.

Baudelaire, C. 1964. *The painter of modern life and other essays*. London: Phaidon.

Baudrillard, J. 1983. *Simulations*. New York: Semiotext(e).

Berman, M. 1983. *All that is solid melts into air*. London: Verso.

Calvino, I. 1978. *Invisible cities*. London: Picador.

Castells, M, 1977. *The urban question*. London: Edward Arnold.

Castells, M. 1983. *The city and the grass roots*. London: Edward Arnold.

Cooke, P. (ed.) 1989. *Localities*. London: Unwin Hyman.

Derrida, J. 1978. *Writing and difference*. London: Routledge & Kegan Paul.

Durkheim, E. 1983. *The division of labour*. London: Macmillan.

Dworkin, R. 1986. *Law's empire*. London: Fontana.

Foster, J. 1974. *Class struggle and the industrial revolution*. London: Methuen.

Foucault, M. 1980. *Power/Knowledge*. New York: Pantheon.

Frankel, B. 1987. *The Post-industrial utopians*. Cambridge: Polity.

Frankenberg, R. (ed.) 1967. *Communities in Britain*. Harmondsworth: Penguin.

Geddes, P. 1940. *Cities in evolution*. London: Williams & Norgate.

Gellner, E. 1983. *Nations and nationalism*. London: Weidenfeld & Nicolson.

Gorz, A. 1985. *Paths to paradise*. London: Pluto.

Gramsci, A. 1971. *Selections from the prison notebooks*. London: Lawrence & Wishart.

Howard, E. 1960. *Garden cities of tomorrow*, London: Faber.

Habermas, J. 1985. Modernity – an incomplete project. In *Postmodern culture*, H. Foster (ed.). London: Pluto 3–15.

Habermas, J. 1987. *The philosophical discourse of modernity*. Cambridge: Polity.

Harvey, D. 1982. *The limits to capital*. Oxford: Basil Blackwell.

Hewison, R. 1987. *The heritage industry*. London: Methuen.

Hobsbawm, E. & T. Ranger 1983. *The invention of tradition*. Cambridge: Cambridge University Press.

Hughes, R. 1980. *The shock of the new*. London: BBC Publications.

Hutcheon, L. 1988. *A poetics of postmodernism*. London: Routledge.

Jameson, F. 1985. Postmodernism and consumer society. In *Postmodern culture*. H. Foster (ed.), London: Pluto, 111–125.

Keynes, J.M. 1937. *The general theory of employment, interest and money*. London: Macmillan.

Kuhn, T. 1967. *The structure of scientific revolutions*. Chicago: Chicago University Press.

Le Play, F. 1855. *Les ouvriers européens*. Paris: Presses universitaires.

References

Lipietz, A. 1987. *Mirages and miracles*. London: Verso.

Littler, C. 1982. *The development of the labour process in capitalist societies*. London: Heinemann.

Lyotard, J.-F. 1984. *The postmodern condition*. Manchester: Manchester University Press.

Marshall, A. 1919. *Industry and trade*. London: Macmillan.

Marx, K. 1976. *Capital*, 3 vols. Harmondsworth: Penguin.

Marx, K. & F. Engels 1968. *The German ideology*. Moscow: Progress.

McHale, B. 1987. *Postmodernist fiction*. London: Methuen.

Nairn, T. 1981. *The break-up of Britain*. London: Verso.

O'Hagan, T. 1984. *The end of law?* Oxford: Basil Blackwell.

Pahl, R. 1975. *Whose city?* Harmondsworth: Penguin.

Piore, M. & C. Sabel 1984. *The second industrial divide*. New York: Basic Books.

Pynchon, T. 1980. *Gravity's rainbow*. London: Picador.

Rawls, J. 1973. *A theory of justice*. Oxford: Oxford University Press.

Rorty, R. 1980. *Philosophy and the mirror of nature*. Oxford: Basil Blackwell.

Smith, A. 1979. *The wealth of nations*. Harmondsworth: Penguin.

Taylor, F. 1913. *The principles of scientific management*. New York: Harper & Row.

Thompson, H.S. 1972. *Fear and loathing in Las Vegas*. London: Paladin.

Tönnies, F. 1971. *Selected writings*. Chicago: Harcourt, Brace, Jovanovic.

Unger, R. 1984. *Passion: an essay on personality*. New York: Basic Books.

Weber, M. 1980. *Economy and society*. New York: Bedminster Press.

Williams, G. 1978. *The Merthyr rising*. London: Croom Helm.

Williams, R. 1983. *Towards 2000*. London: Chatto & Windus.

INDEX

housing schemes 105–6
urban social movement 45
Frankel, B. 138–9
Frankenberg, R. 36
freedom, concepts of 49,
50, 52, 88
French Revolution 5, 12
post-Revolutionary
experiences 5–6
Fuentes, C. 101

Geddes, P. 34–5
Gellner, E. 20
General Motors 75
production diversity
64–5, 148
Germany 19, 21, 60
West 80, 81, 141, 165
global markets and
economy 29, 115, 129,
141, 171, 172
Goethe, J.W. von 10
Gorz, A. 138
Gramsci, A. 24
Graves, M. 103, 108
Great Britain
construction industry 72
economic problems 81
economic structure 121
Ford Motor Company
investment 73–5, 82
increased central
controls 116, 129–30
labour controls 118
labour "social contract"
72
local enterprise 174–5
localities study 120–30
monetarist strategies 82,
118
planned production
methods 61
trade union curbs 82
welfare state provision
68
see also England;
Northern Ireland;
Scotland; Wales
Greece 165
Greek culture 4
guild system 35, 59

Habermas, J. 4, 51, 93, 94

Harvey, D. 75
Haussmann, Baron 15, 26
Hegel, G.W.F. 48–9
heritage, decline of 53–4
heterotopia 100
history
as aestheticization of
everyday life 54–7
loss in postmodernism
109–11, 112
traditional presentation
of 52–3
Hobsbawm, E. 21
housing
for Ford car workers 73
in industrial cities 25
mass 71
public sector 70–1, 82–3,
105–6, 179
Rietveld Schroder House
85
subsidies 70, 72, 77
suburban 28
Howard, E. 34
Hughes, R. 9
Hutcheon, L. 101–2, 108,
112

imports, impact of 158, 159
incentives, five-dollar day
63–4
income levels 68, 160
industrial communities
37–8
industrial districts 143,
164–8
industrial organization and
development 59–61
spatial strategies 73–5
Industrial Revolution 12
industrialization 25–6
inflation 158
and income levels 68, 81
and stagnation 80
combating strategies 81
infrastructure
development 77
inner-city problems 123,
178
interdisciplinary
crossovers 97
international technology
transfer 172

through municipal authority 26,
27
social protest, Paris, May 1968 45
social solidarity 31–2
of localities 130–1
social systems
rural 3
town and county divisions 23, 24
see also localities
society
pluralistic 180
polarization of 119–20, 130, 157–8,
160
theories of 30–3, 47, 111, 138–9
sociology, as response to modernity
30
South America, industrial
investment 78
South-East Asia 81
as cheap labour market 78–9
sovereignty 47–8
consumer 84
Soviet Union 136
in global market 172
internal reassessment initiatives
138, 142
need for technology 172
regional identity assertion 132
space
decentralized problem-free
125
industrial 73–9
in modern urban environments
13, 26–7
of paradox 100
Spain 18, 19, 78, 141, 165
Basque movement 20
Bilbao 25
state
intervention, effect on localism
127–8
regulation of capitalist
development process 75–6, 76–7
regulatory intervention 67
subsidies for industrial
investment 76–7
suburbia 27–8, 37
surrealism 16
Sweden 142
Switzerland 142
symbols 21
synthesis, of past and future 20, 21,
22, 37

Taylor, F., scientific management of
work 60
technological change
impact on construction industry
72
impact on labour market 138, 158
impact on production methods
61, 154–7
territorial expansion and
boundaries, 17, 18
economic influences 18–9
effects on mobility 18
Terry, Q. 87, 104
Thackeray, W.M. 12
Thatcher, M. 131, 133, 142
Thatcherism 116–17, 118, 127
"throw-away society" 3, 111
time and space, concepts of 13, 111,
175
Tonnies, F. 31, 47–8
tourism industry 126–7
trade policies and development,
and expansionism 19
trades unions
curbs 82, 118, 159
early 24
erosion of local influence 127
Ford Company 63
in Fordist organizations 162
in Japanese companies 153
tradition 21, 86
authority of 87
transportation systems
impact on urbanization and
industrialization 27-8
truth
and exercising of power 96
and experience 89
Turkey 142

unemployment 83, 125–6
combating strategies 69
Unger, R. 51, 52, 114
United States of America
crossborder economic integration
142
industrial districts 165
local economic development 175
polarization 157
postmodern architecture 106, 107
public development authorities
176
studies of community power 43

Index